*Hooked by Fly Fishing.*        Graham M. Mott

# Hooked

# by

# Fly Fishing

## Feel-Good Stories
## of Family and Friends,
## Life Lessons,
## Mishaps, and Mayhem

## Graham M. Mott

# Hooked by Fly Fishing

## Graham M. Mott

## Copyright ©2024

Golden Shadows Press

Photos of "parachute Adams" from www.catalog.theflyshop.com and Free clipart images courtesy of gosvgdesign.blogspot.com, canstock.com, canstockphoto.com, clipartguy.com, coolclips.com, vectorcartoons.com, DennisCoxclipartof.com, illustrationsof.com, bigstockphoto.com, vectorstock.com, pingart.com, shutterstock.com, retraclipart.com, and adobe.com.
.

Attention non-profit organizations, clubs, schools, and more: quantity discounts are available at the author's cost plus shipping for sales promotions or fundraising. Custom imprinting of logos or company name on the cover is possible. For more information, contact Graham M. Mott, Golden Shadows Press, grahammott@hotmail.com or call 720-278-1959.

# Table of Contents

# Dedication

I want to mention the most important people in my life:

First to my son, Writer Mott, who I shared so many memorable, wonderful, and amazing days while fly fishing. I am lucky to have such a special relationship with him, and so proud of him as he is a such a caring and successful person.

To the spirit of my beautiful daughter, Kristine Johnson, who passed away in 2001 at the age of 30 from brain cancer. Her life lives on through her two children, Ris Johnson and Rider Johnson.

To my wife, DeAnne, who has always been the love and light of my life. She is beautiful, but her real beauty lies beneath the surface. She is out-going, smart, creative, intuitive, gracious, empathetic, and positive and has taught me much about the spiritual side of my life. Many times, she sat patiently reading a book for hours next to a river while I lost all sense of time casting to waiting trout.

To my mother, Aimee` Graham Mott, who was always there for me. She was the glue that kept our whole family together. Special thanks to her for collecting and saving my father's and his ancestors' stories for me.

To my father, John Grenville Mott, who I called by the nickname "Ghin." He was a newspaper sportswriter with a byline "Beyond the Pail" and occasionally wrote about flyfishing in New Mexico. Eventually, he opened the first public relations firm in El Paso, Texas. Thanks for his love of sports and writing which he passed on to me.

To my stepson, J.D. Frette, who I nicknamed "Bubs." He joined me for several memorable flyfishing adventures. I am so proud of him and consider him my son.

To my sister, Sheridan Hansen, brother-in-law Jon Hansen, and favorite nephew Tom Hansen for their support and generosity.

To Hal Writer, who first introduced me to the sport of fly fishing at the Wigwam Club. He was a great mentor and spiritual guide and treated me like his son.

To my best friend Jim Hastedt, and other buddies, Bob Sherr, Ken Decker, and D. J. "Sandy" Colling who shared many pleasant times fly fishing with me.

# Acknowledgements

I would like to recognize a few other family members and friends:

First is to my great grandfather, John G. Mott, also known as "Eagle Father," who wrote a detailed diary about his big game hunting trip from Chicago to Wyoming in 1900.

Second to my grandfather, Russell Mott, who was a big game hunter and sportsman, for his stories published in *Forest and Stream Magazine* using the pseudonym "Double Barrel." He was also a fly fisherman.

Third to my mother's brother, Ed Graham, who was an advertising executive and cartoonist for the Saturday Evening Post, New Yorker Magazine, and other publications. I used one of his cartoon characters depicting a man sitting in a chair reading a book as the logo for my publishing company, Golden Shadows Press.

Fourth to Alan Larson, who taught me his easy hook extraction method, and Gary "Goose" Goldsberry, who gave me his meticulously tied fly collection.

And finally, to my grandson, Keen Schledorn-Mott, for all his technical assistance creating my book cover, helping to format my book for self-publishing and filming videos for marketing and social media.

# Introduction

In this book, I have reflected on my life as a fly fisherman. Through a traumatic childhood, an alcoholic father, a painful divorce, a stepfamily, and my daughter's death, these events set me on a remarkable journey of discovery and recovery. During my lifetime of both pain and loss, I have learned so many valuable lessons about love, forgiveness, and empathy. I realized these personal happenings were a gift to me.

Introduced to flyfishing by my father-in-law, I found a wonderful sport to help me deal with my anger and forgive my father's alcohol addiction. Spending so many hours on a river or stream was like a cool salve for my woundedness. I meditated as the waters flowed around me like a healing balm.

My mother saved a diary and magazine articles by my father's relatives who were outdoorsmen, hunters and fly fishermen. This information brought me full circle to uncovering and recovering my past. My great grandfather,

grandfather, and father were all writers. Suddenly, a new world opened to me when I discovered I also loved to write.

Graham M. Mott

# Chapter 1

# Fly Fishing Heaven

*"During the next hour's fishing,*
*I saw my fly line suddenly shudder,*
*felt a hard strike, raised the rod, set the hook,*
*and stared wide-eyed*
*as a large rainbow trout*
*jumped and raced downstream."*

Can you possibly imagine where my first fly fishing experience took place? My father-in-law, Hal introduced me to the sport. When I met him, we hit it off immediately as he had three daughters and no sons. Little did I know that Hal was very successful in Denver business. He was in his early 70's when I met him, but I never thought about his age as he was so active and healthy. Hal was short, thin, and bald but his strong, assured, and friendly personality made his stature seem much bigger in everyone's eyes. From the beginning, I felt a special kinship with him. Since I didn't have a close relationship with my own father, it was a natural evolution to feel good about an older male who took an interest in me. He loved golf, playing cards, flyfishing and duck hunting.

One day while talking with Hal, he asked if I had an interest in learning to fly fish. Enthusiastically, I told him I would love to learn the sport. Hal told me he was a member of a private fly-fishing club on the South Platte River and would like to have me join him. Being naïve and newer to the Denver area, I had no idea Hal was talking about one of the most exclusive fly-fishing clubs in Colorado. Little did I know that only the wealthy, elite, and privileged were voted in as members of this select club, and only a small number of members and guests ever had the opportunity to fish this special property.

I jumped at the chance to spend more time with Hal and learn as much as I could from him. When the day arrived for our first fishing excursion, I was excited and could hardly wait to go. We left Denver about 8:30 in the morning, and I drove Hal's Cadillac south to the small town of Sedalia and turned west following a two-lane dirt road into the mountains and eventually arrived overlooking the South Platte River. At around 10am, I looked down from the road above the entrance to the Wigwam Club and spotted several cabins and buildings along the shore of the river just below Cheesman Canyon.

It was an idyllic place where the river itself had been sculptured with well-placed large boulders providing pool after pool of perfect habitat and holding areas for trout. There were also several diversionary canals next to the river where both rainbow and German brown trout were raised from small fry to at least one or two pounds to be eventually stocked in the river.

As I was viewing the Wigwam Club, Hal pointed out the uppermost pool situated just below the public Cheesman Canyon water and told me the story about an exceptionally large German brown trout that made its home in that location.

The fish had been named "Gus" and most of the members, from one time or another, had attempted to catch this trophy-sized fish. A few had even been lucky enough to hook "Gus," but no one could ever land the prize. This trout was like a Paul Bunyan figure, bigger than life, and its reputation had reached epic proportions. "Gus" weighed from five to ten pounds and was a brown trout that fly fisherman could only dream about landing once during a lifetime.

Hal told me the Wigwam members had tried many different techniques including night fishing with large streamer flies to try to entice this behemoth. Gus was a legendary fish, and its stature continued to grow bigger year after year. One night, a non-member fisherman situated in the public water above the pool and fishing a spinning rod using a large piece of sucker meat as bait, let his line drift under the fence dividing the public property from the Wigwam Club. To the Wigwam members' obvious dismay, he hooked "Gus" and eventually netted the king-sized German brown trout and took his prize home. As the story goes, there has never been a larger trout caught in the South Platte River near Deckers, Colorado.

At the time, I was excited to be visiting the Wigwam Club but didn't realize how significant it was to have my first fly fishing experience at this elite location until a few years later. I knew something special was taking place but at the time could not get my mind around it. I drove through the entrance to the club and down the narrow road parking the car next to a cabin with a sign "Bachelors" above the front door. It was aptly named for the members and guests who came to fish without their wives or families.

Hal provided me with all the fishing gear I would need. Included were thick Hodgeman rubber chest waders with suspenders and attached felt-soled boots, a three-piece bamboo fly rod, a single action Hardy reel, a fishing vest, a net, some gut leaders, and a fly box with various beautifully tied flies.

Even though I was twenty-five years old, I couldn't help feeling giddy and like a little kid who was going to the "candy store" for the first time. Hal, who was in no hurry, made me take my time putting on my gear as he slowly and methodically pulled on his waders. Since I was his guest and totally reliant on his training and tutelage, I had no choice but to take some deep breaths to help slow myself down. As I was to learn from several excursions to the Wigwam Club, Hal only fly fished for an hour or so, never expended any extra energy, waded in shallow water close to shore, and showed his skills by catching a large rainbow trout. He was truly remarkable and an expert wet-fly fisherman.

Due to the intricacies and difficulties of learning the art of casting a fly rod correctly and presenting a fly properly, Hal worked diligently with me for over an hour teaching me to tie knots, choosing various flies to attach to my gut leader, and showing me how to cast the rod and retrieve the fly. He pointed out the water where trout would likely be located and had me practice wading in the river. It was a crash course, and like an overeager kid, I was impatient to try what he had taught me.

Hal could not contain my youthful enthusiasm. Finally, it was time to get my feet wet. We walked to the river's edge for my first fly fishing endeavor. I was using Hal's two wet-fly fishing method including a larger streamer fly, the muddler minnow, and a smaller royal coachman. I followed his instructions by casting both flies across the river at a forty-five-degree angle, letting the flies sink under the water, allowing the line to move downstream eventually straightening out, and retrieving my fly line in short stripping motions. He told me I could expect a strike at any time my flies were in the water. Hal couldn't help smiling while watching me attempt to cast my rod without snagging one of my flies in a bush nearby or snapping one off during my back cast.

Time passed quickly and the lunch bell rang so it was time to take a break and stop fishing. Of course, I wanted to catch my first trout and had no appetite for food, but my only choice was to join Hal for lunch. Wolfing down my food as quickly as possible, it was agonizing as I watched Hal slowly chew and swallow each morsel from his plate. Patience was not one of my stronger virtues. I found myself daydreaming as I looked out the picture window at the river. As soon as Hal finished his meal, I excused myself, ran back to "Batchelors," pulled on my waders, grabbed my fly rod, and headed for the river.

During the next hour's fishing, I saw my fly line suddenly shudder, felt a hard strike, raised the rod, set the hook, and stared wide-eyed as a large rainbow trout jumped and raced downstream. I knew at that exact moment I was "hooked by fly fishing." Shouting at Hal to get his attention, I felt adrenalin surge through me as I fought my first trout on a fly rod.

Hal lived to be 90 years old and didn't quit fishing until his early eighties. He probably took me at least twenty times to fish the Wigwam Club, but of course, I could never go enough. His generosity also included taking his other grandsons, two of my friends, and my sister's family as guests to fish the club.

Hal and I never stayed at the club for more than four hours at a time as he wanted to get back to the Denver Country Club by mid-afternoon to gamble playing gin rummy. Of course, I would have preferred to miss lunch and fish. Sometimes, I would even try to hide behind a bush when Hal drove along the river looking for me to join him.

Using Hal's two-wet-fly method, I was lucky enough to experience hooking two trout almost simultaneously two times. When you hook two fish, your fly line is pulled in sudden, erratic directions making it feel as if you are fighting something surreal. Seeing two trout jump makes your heart skip a beat as you can hardly believe this event can be happening to you. Hooking two fish didn't just happen to me at the Wigwam Club, but I also had that same experience while fishing the Blue River not far below Dillon Reservoir and the White River near Budge's Resort. This was such a magical happening, and I equated it to a golfer making a hole in one. It has been many years since I had that experience.

While visiting the Wigwam Club, I also taught myself how to fish dry flies and eventually spent much of my time looking for rising trout. The first time almost happened by accident when I spied a fish rising at the top of a pool. I changed flies and tied on an Adams dry fly and caught a beautiful rainbow on my first cast. The Adams became my favorite until a few years later when I started using the parachute Adams. I wouldn't say that moment made me a dry fly purist, but after that experience, I always preferred casting to rising trout.

In 1978, Hal offered to nominate my name for membership in the Wigwam Club. It was quite an honor. To say I was pleased was an understatement as I had never dreamed of becoming a member. Most of the members were wealthy retired gentlemen. The cost of membership included a fee of $10,000 or more plus annual dues and daily usage costs for the cabins, meals, and guests. For me, it was a pipe dream to be considered for membership at this premier fishing club. Hal was especially popular among the members and didn't have a son so I figured it was a possibility that his cronies might approve my membership. To put it mildly, I was so flattered to even be considered among such prominent people.

Simultaneously, my marriage to his daughter ended. Being realistic, the club's cost of membership was beyond my financial means, and since my marriage had dissolved, I knew the possibility of becoming a member was over. Hal and I never talked about membership again.

I stopped by Hal's home on his 90th birthday and thanked him for all his support and teaching me to fly fish.

He passed away a few months later from a stroke while playing gin rummy with his buddies at the Denver Country Club.

From time to time, I still try to visualize what it would have been like to be a member of one of the pre-eminent fly-fishing clubs. While I was lucky enough to fish the Wigwam Club numerous times, the whole experience was so perfect that most other fishing locales paled by comparison. Realistically, being a member of the Wigwam Club did not really fit me. Like all my Mott ancestors, I am unpretentious, a renegade, an individualist, and have no interest in being a member of any club.

Thanks to Hal for introducing me to fly fishing. Sometimes when arriving at the South Platte River near Deckers, I park my car above the Wigwam Club and gaze down upon "fly fishing heaven."

Next: **In the Lip**

Cartoon by Hohenbrink

"Looks like a group of first-time fly fishermen."

---

# Chapter 2

# In the Lip

*"Soon the canyon clouded over,*
*and the wind increased*
*making it especially difficult*
*to cast two flies, but I wasn't going*
*to let the breezy conditions*
*deter me from fishing."*

---

To say that I was obsessed with fly fishing after my indoctrination at the Wigwam Club was an understatement. Whenever there was a free moment to get away and go fishing during the week, I usually went by myself but did have my wife's nephews, Jamie and Peter, join me on a couple of occasions. One day I drove to the Cheesman Canyon parking lot and hiked for twenty minutes up the hill and then down the steep path into the canyon above the Wigwam Club.

After arriving at the river, I decided to use Hal's two-wet-fly method. At the time, I picked his favorite streamer, a muddler minnow, and attached a Rio Grande king as the dropper fly. The canyon walls were bathed in both sun and shade on this warm day. The South Platte River was wider at the bottom and gradually narrowed into deeper pools as it progressed upstream a mile or so to the dam at the Cheesman Reservoir. This stretch always intrigued me as I could look down on the deeper pools and see large trout holding in the slower water. These fish were selective and not as easy to catch as the stockers at the Wigwam Club.

Fishing for the first hour or so, I managed to hook only one trout and with a big jump and head-jerk, it threw my fly. Soon the canyon totally clouded over, and the wind increased making it more difficult to cast two flies, but I wasn't going to let the breezy conditions deter me from fishing.

As I was attempting to pick up my line on a back cast, my dropper fly, a size #14 Rio Grande king, hit my face and lodged its barb on the right side in the fatty tissue just below my lower lip. I tried to pull the fly out myself but could not see what I was doing. The barb of the hook was stuck quite deeply, and there was no possibility of removing it myself. I used my clippers to remove the leader where it was attached to the eye of the hook.

Eventually, I met another fisherman who I asked for help, but he didn't feel comfortable attempting to pull the fly out below my lip. Instead, he suggested I find a doctor to remove it.

Being a diehard fly fisherman, I wasn't ready to end my day, so kept fishing for another two hours. My lip only throbbed slightly. I was able to catch a couple of trout during the afternoon. Finally, I decided it was time to leave the river if I was going to make the drive to Denver and see my doctor at the Littleton Clinic before 5pm.

When I walked into the medical office and a full waiting room of ten or more people, I felt self-conscious with a black fly dangling below my lower lip. Imagine my embarrassment as I tried to quietly explain my predicament to the receptionist while the people sitting nearby listened to our conversation. I pointed at the fly and told her I needed the services of a doctor to remove it. Since I had no appointment, I would be the last patient. Time passed slowly, and I noticed a few stares at my new facial decoration, but thankfully, no one mentioned it. With today's fad of body piercings, this lip decoration would be no big deal, but obviously, this incident happened many years earlier.

Later, the doctor gave me a shot of Novocain, removed the fly material, cut the eyelet from the hook, and pushed the barb and hook back through the inside of my lip. My lower lip bled slightly and was swollen, but it was a relatively painless and simple procedure. I made the right choice to have a doctor remove the hook.

Remembering Hal's advice about being extra-careful casting two flies and always wearing sunglasses to protect my eyes during windy conditions, I told myself that I would be much more cautious when casting two flies next time.

Guess what happened next? Obviously, I hadn't learned my previous lesson well enough because I hooked myself again less than a year later fishing two flies during windy conditions on the Blue River above Dillon Reservoir.

This time, I managed to stick the dropper fly, a size #16 red and white royal coachman, deeply in the top of my right ear with an errant back cast. It was definitely déjà vu as I found myself visiting the same doctor with a fashionable new earring. I noticed his bemused look as I once again explained my problem. After extracting the fly, the doctor asked me with a wry smile if I planned to see him again. We both laughed, but I couldn't find much humor at my expense. Each medical procedure was an expensive lesson for me.

Those moments were humbling for me. I had to swallow my pride because I thought I was an accomplished fly caster. It was obvious I still had many lessons to learn. It is inevitable if you fish often that you will probably stick a hook in yourself. Since then, like many other fly fishermen, I have also hooked flies in my vest, net, shirt, boots, and laces, but thankfully, I never needed a doctor's assistance to remove one "in the lip."

Next: **Hooking a Lunker**

# Chapter 3

# Hooking a Lunker

---

*"My heart raced as I was sure*
*I had hooked a huge trout*
*as I never felt a fish this strong.*
*It rapidly stripped the line off my reel.*
*There was no possibility*
*of stopping such a big fish."*

---

Y ou may know that wonderful feeling when first viewing a valley that is so beautiful it almost takes your breath away. That is how I felt when I first laid my eyes on the South Fork of the White River curving among beaver ponds and nestled in a lush valley with forests and tall rugged mountains on both sides. It was a five-hour road trip from Denver to the river driving I-70 to the exit next to the Colorado River at Gypsum and a long winding steep climb along a narrow dirt road up the mountainside to a high plateau. The rest of the trip included driving through aspen groves and meadows while crossing several small streams until finally dropping back down in the White River valley on a steep, rocky, and rutted road. The latter part of the trip was slow going but well worth it when you finally arrived. In fact, one time while driving down this road toward the White River, I managed to high center my car and had to walk for several miles to summon help.

Besides camping near the river, there was only one other place to stay, Budges Lodge, built in 1931. This resort is now called Budge's Flattops Wilderness Lodge and consists of a dining hall and seven primitive log cabins in a serene setting close to the White River and adjacent to the Flat Tops Wilderness Area in the White River National Forest, and 40 miles from the nearest paved road. Guest cabins were lighted by kerosene lamps and heated with wood stoves. There was a sink and a toilet in each cabin with only a shower curtain around it for privacy and an outside cold communal shower. This resort offered daily meals and horseback rides or pack trips to fish back country lakes in the wilderness area. It was a better than camping out, and the food was good, family-style fare.

My father-in-law, Hal told me about this resort. I traveled to Budges several times during the next few years with my sister's family and other friends.

The White River was a small clear stream that consisted of beautifully colored nine-to-twelve-inch wild brook trout that were fun to catch. These brookies rose readily to the dry fly, and if you waded carefully, you could also fish the beaver ponds or other smaller creeks located adjacent to the river.

One morning, I remember watching hypnotized as an older gentleman made beautiful long fly casts while he was standing on the shore of the river near a foot bridge. His casting action was so graceful, and he lightly picked his line off the river, played it out behind him and shot it back toward the far bank of the river. During one cast, I witnessed an amazing site. As the fisherman's line shot forward and played out almost like magic, his fishing fly and a bird met in mid-air, and suddenly the hooked bird flew off with his line and landed in a nearby bush. Fortunately, I was able to offer help, grabbed his fly line, pulled the bird to me, and removed the fly from its back. The bird was not seriously injured and flew off.

I had recently purchased a two-piece Orvis "Trouter" 6-foot, 5 or 6 weight graphite fly rod and added an Orvis lightweight fly reel with six-pound floating fly line. Graphite was the latest material to be used for fly rod blanks and revolutionized the sport. My Orvis rod was slow-action, and it took some time to get used to casting it, but I loved its power and flexibility.

During one of my visits to Budges, I decided to fish a weighted muddler minnow through a long deep pool adjacent to a dammed beaver pond. I made a cast to the opposite side of the river and let my leader and fly sink deeply and carried slowly downstream. As my slack line played out, it was time to start stripping the muddler back toward me. During my retrieve, I saw a large boil in the river, felt my rod recoil with a hard strike, and set the hook. My heart raced as I was sure I had hooked a huge trout as I never felt a fish this strong. It rapidly stripped the line off my reel.

There was no possibility of stopping such a big fish. Trying to decide how I might manage to land this trout; I scrambled out of the river and ran down the shore after it. It was just a matter of a few more seconds before I finally glimpsed this lunker, and my muddler minnow snapped off my leader. I looked in rapt amazement and laughed to myself when I realized I had not hooked a trout at all, but rather an extremely angry beaver. For a few moments, that beaver had me believing I might have hooked the largest trout ever caught on the White River.

In fact, it was not my only encounter with beavers. During a few other late afternoons or early evenings, I stood on the dam of a beaver pond waving off the mosquitoes and casting my dry fly to rising brookies. It was fun to see the beavers swimming nearby and loudly slapping their tails as a warning to exit their territory.

It has been many years since I visited Budges, but I doubt that much has changed. Although with the population explosion in Colorado, I am sure the river has much more fishing pressure now. The Colorado Game and Fish designated the White River as a Gold Medal stream with flies and lures only and catch and release restrictions. This beautiful wilderness area will always hold a special place in my heart as I recall "hooking a lunker."

Next: **Lure of Montana**

# Chapter 4

# Lure of Montana

---

*"There were a few salmon flies*
*floating on the Madison River.*
*It was interesting to watch*
*these big insects gyrate on the surface*
*until an occasional trout rose*
*and gulped down a tempting morsel."*

---

In 1975, I became good friends with a new real estate agent in my Denver Tech Center office. Jim was my age and from a small town, Columbus, near the coast of Texas, had attended the Air Force Academy and loved to hunt and fish. I was the one who peaked Jim's interest in fly fishing and even bought him his first fly rod, an Orvis "Trouter," like the one I already owned.

I think it may have been Jim's idea that we take a five-day fly-fishing trip to Montana and float the fabled Madison River. We made our travel plans to fly Frontier Airlines to West Yellowstone, Montana in July, rent a car and drive to the Madison. Both of us were hoping our trip would coincide with this river's famous "salmon fly" hatch. Since Jim didn't own chest waders, I lent him my extra pair.

Jim and I were excited as we boarded the Frontier turbo-prop airplane for the mid-afternoon flight to West Yellowstone. Airlines' regulations would not allow us to carry our aluminum rod cases onto the plane and required checking our rods and duffle bags as baggage.

After exiting the plane in West Yellowstone, I watched carefully as a Frontier employee unloaded the plane's baggage compartment while it feathered its engines. I was nervous since I could never see our bags or rods. After ten minutes, the plane quickly departed for Idaho.

I am sure you can guess what happened next. I knew our fishing gear was not on the tarmac and complained to the Frontier Airlines agent about the problem. He kept insisting that all the bags and rods had been unloaded before departure, but eventually had to admit Frontier's mistake.

As the return plane flight from Idaho would not arrive back in West Yellowstone until the next day at noon, we were both quite upset. I am sure you can imagine our chagrin as we realized that we were losing almost a full day's fishing due to Frontier's mistake. The only concession the agent made was paying for our dinners. We rented a car, stopped at a restaurant, and checked into a motel for the night.

Despite our frustration, Jim and I decided to make the best of our circumstance. If our bags arrived at noon tomorrow, we could still be fishing the fabled Madison River by mid-to-late afternoon.

We had made reservations with a guide service to float the Madison in two days. I phoned our guide, Doug, who told us the salmon fly hatch was in its waning stages. He said there were still a few big bugs on the water, and the good news included the possibility of catching a caddis hatch.

At noon, Jim and I arrived at the airport, grabbed our bags and rods, and drove toward the Madison River. Our exhilaration mounted as the road paralleled the Gallatin River, a smaller picturesque stream. It looked so inviting that Jim suggested we stop and make a few casts. To save time, we didn't put on our waders but instead, set up our Orvis fly rods and cast Adams dry flies into the current while standing on large boulders overlooking the river. On Jim's second or third cast, he hooked a colorful twelve-inch rainbow trout. Soon, I also had a fish take my fly. Jim and I were giddy about our good luck. Despite our quick success, we decided to leave the Gallatin and drive to fish the Madison.

Driving past Hebgen Lake, we stopped at a resort with small cabins located adjacent to the river. After renting a cabin for the night, stashing our bags, donning our waders, and assembling our rods, we started wading and fly fishing. Soon I was casting to waiting trout, felt a strike but quickly lost the fish.

As I was concentrating on my fly's presentation, I noticed that Jim had waded out of the river and was walking directly toward me. He stopped nearby and told me the waders that I lent him were leaking water. The hole had enlarged and was not repairable. His pants and socks were soaked. Jim would have to drive back to West Yellowstone to purchase a new pair of chest waders.

What a dilemma for me: go with Jim to get waders or stay to flyfish for trout? What should I do? Of course, I couldn't imagine not fishing so I told Jim to drive the rental car to West Yellowstone. Though it was my fault he had leaky waders, I could see no reason why both of us should lose quality fishing time on the Madison. After all, we had already lost almost a full day's fishing. If you had been in my place, what would you have done?

Remembering the situation now, I probably should have been more empathetic to my friend and joined him on his drive to buy new waders. At the time, I was unconcerned about Jim's plight. My total focus was on fly fishing, and there was no chance I was leaving the river. If I could do it all over again, I would like to think that I might have been a bigger person. In hindsight, I don't blame Jim for being frustrated with me because if the situation had been reversed, I might have felt the same way, but I seriously doubt it. I am sure I would have left Jim so he could continue fishing and made the drive by myself to purchase new waders. Not making any excuses, it seems as if most fly fishermen have tunnel vision as fishing totally consumes their thoughts, and catching fish is the only goal no matter what else occurs.

I felt I could justify my position for three good reasons: First, we had already lost valuable stream time.

Second, only one person had to make the drive to buy new waders. Third, one of us could continue to fish. I felt I had explained my reasoning by covering all the bases. Do you agree?

Now it is easy to say that my friendship with Jim was more important than staying to fly fish. After all, if Jim had known in advance about my leaky waders, he would have bought himself a new pair before leaving Denver. Did it really make a big difference to have a couple of extra hours fishing for wild trout on the Madison River? At the time, I knew it was worth it. Hindsight is 20-20. Do you agree with my reasoning?

Eventually Jim returned with new waders, and we both caught a few trout before nightfall. We laughed and joked about our day, but I could not understand why Jim was still upset with me. I rationalized that nothing could be better than fly fishing for trout on the Madison River.

A year or so later, I apologized to Jim for not being more considerate since I had caused his leaky wader problem. However, I still doubted whether I would have handled the situation any differently.

The lesson repeated itself a few years later when I offered to lend another pair of waders to a realtor friend named Dwaine. He was not a happy camper when he returned from his first fly fishing outing. You can just imagine the cuss words emanating from Dwaine's mouth as he told me about wading into the river for the first time, and the shock that went through him as he felt the icy cold water around his leg and crotch. I could not believe I had repeated the "holey waders" episode a second time. I was truly sorry about Dwaine's misfortune but couldn't help laughing to myself as I visualized the scene he described so vividly. I am glad this experience did not deter Dwaine from continuing to fly fish. Finally learning my lesson, I never again lent waders to anyone else. I believe, in both instances, I had conveniently forgotten to repair previous leaks.

On our second day, Jim and I drove down the river and looked at Quake Lake, an eerie and stark looking geological formation. Early that afternoon, we noticed some trout rising in a slow-moving pool on a bend of the Madison. Not being sure what kind of bugs were attracting the activity, we decided to fish our favorite and most reliable dry fly, the Adams. It didn't take long for us to start hooking fish. Jim and I loved fly fishing within a few feet of each other while catching trout after trout that rose to our flies. We each caught a half dozen fish before the hot action ended. Practicing catch and release, we carefully removed our flies so each trout could be caught another day. Being competitive, Jim and I had already made a bet on who would catch the most trout during our trip. We both had high expectations about our float trip the next day.

Up early at dawn, Jim and I eagerly drove to meet Doug at the appointed put-in spot on the Madison, a mile or so below Quake Lake. When we arrived, Doug had already placed his "McKenzie" drift boat in the water. He told us we would be floating approximately seven miles. We donned our waders, set up our rods and reels, climbed into his boat, shoved off, and started drifting down the river by 8:30am. Jim stood in the front of the boat while I was stationed in the back. A few large salmon flies floated by us from time to time. We watched these big bugs gyrate on the water's surface until an occasional trout would rise and gulp down the tempting morsels. Doug worked hard rowing and holding the boat in prime casting spots near rising fish so Jim and I could make decent casts. The morning float was uneventful with Jim and I catching a few trout, mostly rainbows, using salmon fly imitations.

Stopping for lunch, we relaxed and enjoyed the scenery. What could be better that floating a famous river in Montana and casting to wild trout with dry flies. Jim and I felt we were in nirvana.

Departing again, we noticed a caddis hatch beginning to appear on the river. Suddenly, the caddis flies arrived in a huge cloud, and the trout started rising aggressively. Jim and I had to keep our mouths closed as the bugs were everywhere, landing on us and climbing on our faces and sunglasses. It was a nightmarish situation as this onslaught of bugs was driving us crazy. Our only consolation was that these flies did not bite like mosquitoes. With so many caddis floating on the water, any trout could readily pick and choose its prey. Despite the annoyance, Jim and I cast our Orvis rods using elk hair caddis flies, and occasionally, a hungry trout would pass up a real caddis and seize an imitation instead.

By the time the hatch was over, Jim and I had each caught over twenty trout. We were tired of flogging the water and swatting caddis and felt great about our successful day. Both of us could not stop talking with Doug about the length and size of this incredible hatch.

Since that day, Jim, my son Writer, and I have fished the caddis hatch on the Arkansas River near Salida, Colorado several times, and despite being sizable, it does not compare to the one we witnessed that day on the Madison River.

Jim and I had made a bet on who caught the most fish and found ourselves tied for the total number of trout when we neared the end of our float trip. Since it was our last fishing day, we intensified our efforts to catch one last fish and win the day. Jim hooked a trout within sight of our take-out spot, and it certainly looked as if the spoils of victory were soon to be his. This fish made a deep run around and under the boat. I made every effort to make sure my fly line would not get tangled with Jim's. When the trout swam past my location, Jim approached nearby. I moved to get out of his way, but my fly rod accidentally whacked his fly line.

Can you guess what happened next? At my rod's contact with Jim's line, the trout unhooked itself and was gone with a splash. Jim swore I hit his rod on purpose so I wouldn't lose our bet. Naturally, he was frustrated and looked at me aghast with the thought that I would purposely ruin his victory. I just held up my arms, tried my best to feign innocence and keep myself from smirking. This last fish would have given Jim the victory and a prime rib dinner, but from my perspective, what could be more fitting than to have our Montana fishing competition end in a tie.

There was no way for me to assuage Jim's feelings. In my wildest dreams, I never could have pulled off such an outcome. Let's get real, would I do such a thing to my best friend? Was I capable of purposely knocking his trout loose? I'll let you be the judge.

Jim would never let me forget those two moments: the leaky waders and losing his winning trout. We have had many good laughs reminiscing about those two events. Despite missing most of a full day's fishing on the Madison River, Jim and I still felt the "lure of Montana."

Next: **Lightning Can Strike Twice**

# Chapter 5

# Lightning Can Strike Twice

---

*"The amazing sight included
a small creek which was absolutely
teeming with cutthroat trout.
There were so many that it looked
like the fish were almost stacked
one on top of another."*

---

After our first trip to Montana, Jim and I made plans to return the following summer to fish the waters in Yellowstone National Park. Once again, we decided to fly Frontier Airlines to West Yellowstone, rent a motel room and a car and have three days to explore the park.

The day of our plane flight, Jim and I arrived early to check-in our bags and rods and make sure they were loaded on the Frontier turboprop airplane. Looking out the terminal's windows, we watched our gear being placed into the plane's baggage compartment. Everything looked perfect as our flight left according to schedule, but after flying 30 to 45 minutes, one of the turbo's two engines started sputtering and smoking and was shut down. The pilot announced that we were returning to Denver to make an emergency landing. Fortunately, the plane landed without incident. We patiently waited a couple of hours in the Denver Airport for a substitute plane to arrive to fly us to Montana.

Of course, it felt as if Jim and I were snakebit flying Frontier Airlines. Both of us were still worried, but the airline personnel assured us that all our gear and rods would be on our next flight to Montana. Could a replay be possible? It was a question we did not want to think about as we boarded the next plane to Montana.

Jim and I arrived in West Yellowstone with our rods and bags missing again. Our worst fears had been manifested. A Frontier employee told us that our bags and rods were sitting in the baggage claim area at the Denver airport. No one had told us to recheck them for the next flight. Just like the previous year, all our gear would arrive on the next afternoon's flight.

Jim and I couldn't believe our bad luck and were frustrated to say the least. Frontier Airlines was the enemy. We could not believe any airlines could be so incompetent and knew we would never fly Frontier again. The agent in West Yellowstone felt our wrath and could not assuage our angry feelings. He offered us a ride in his pickup truck into West Yellowstone and had Frontier pay for our dinners and motel room for the night. It was hard to fathom losing another day in fly fishing paradise.

Jim and I spent most of the next day walking around West Yellowstone and talking to employees at several fishing shops about the current fishing conditions. It wasn't a totally wasted day as we learned about a small creek to fish in Yellowstone Park for cutthroat trout. Our duffel bags and rods arrived from Denver on schedule mid-afternoon.

Following the advice of a local guide, Jim and I rose early the next day and drove into Yellowstone Park passing the Fishing Bridge resort near Yellowstone Lake and continued to a specific location near the east entrance to the park. There were signs at the parking area warning about a dangerous grizzly bear in the area, but that didn't stop Jim and I as we felt infallible. During our fast two-mile hike, we continually shouted to keep any bears from approaching us. We eventually found the pristine little creek which flowed into the lake.

The stream was not more than five to ten feet wide in most places. It was an amazing sight as it was filled with cutthroat trout. There were so many fish that the trout were almost stacked one on top of another. The signage nearby stated no fishing was allowed as the cutthroat were spawning. Jim and I followed the creek to where it eventually entered the lake. It was tempting to fish the creek as you could hook a trout on every cast. We tied royal Wulff flies to our leaders, cast onto the lake to some rising fish and hooked and released several beautifully colored and dotted native cutthroat trout.

Later that afternoon as we were leaving to hike back to the car, I just couldn't pass up the temptation to make a cast to so many trout clustered in this creek. It was like looking at a natural fish hatchery since the fish were so plentiful. Making a short cast and watching my fly land on the creek, the water boiled, and I immediately hooked a fish.

As I quickly released the cutthroat, it was easy to rationalize that I hadn't broken a rule, but it was a good lesson for me. Jim and I talked about it, and I decided I would never break the rules again.

This reminded me of the present-day situation where someone dumped a few lake trout into Yellowstone Lake and compromised the eco-system as these trout rapidly reproduced, grew large, and were eating the smaller native Cutthroat trout. Here was a human being making a stupid decision without knowing the far-reaching and potentially devastating effects of his actions.

On our third day, it was cold and rainy as we drove back into the park and fished the Yellowstone River, which is big, wide, and deep. There were many native trout rising in the river. Jim and I didn't catch one trout as we couldn't seem to find an imitation to match the hatch. It was drizzling and cold. Since, we were both chilled and had developed head colds, we left after two hours.

The morning of our last day, we fished the Madison River in the park and only caught a couple of trout. The cool and rainy weather persisted, and since Jim and I felt lousy, we drove back to West Yellowstone around noon, rented a day room at a local motel, and napped until it was time to leave for our late afternoon flight. Ironically, all our bags and fishing gear arrived back in Denver without incident.

In most cases, a second trip to the same location cannot compare with your first visit. This certainly was true of our two trips to Montana, but we did not let our problems with Frontier Airlines affect our good feelings. There was no reason "to cry over spilt milk."

By fishing different locations each time, we still enjoyed ourselves and forgot the day-to-day hassles and stresses of life. The lesson we learned was to drive our own car to the fishing destination next time or make sure we could carry our fly rods and gear onto the airplane because "lightning can strike twice."

Next: **The Tenderfoot**

# Chapter 6

# The Tenderfoot

---

*"If you don't have much experience
wading in a deep fast river, it can be
especially treacherous and difficult."*

---

Have you ever accompanied a good friend fly fishing for the first time? I made this mistake only once. It was one of those experiences my friend, Bob, would never let me forget. One day, I agreed to take him to fish the South Platte River in Cheesman Canyon. Bob was a novice when it came to the sport, so I told myself I was going to fish and not worry about him.

Fishing and wading Cheesman Canyon is a difficult task even for an experienced fly fisherman. The South Platte River was running high that fateful day at around 450 second feet. I warned Bob to be careful wading and fish near shore where it was shallower and easier to keep his footing.

After a short period of time, I successfully waded across the river at its widest point just a few hundred feet above the Wigwam Club. It seemed like it was only a half an hour later when I noticed Bob wading into deeper water. He smiled and waved at me, but I was alarmed watching him move farther into the river's heavy current. Soon the fast-moving water was above Bob's waist. Just to be safe, I had made sure Bob cinched his waders tightly around his chest with a belt. Suddenly, I felt fearful watching Bob float down the middle of the river. When he reached a shallower portion below him, he was able to drag himself onto shore. I was glad Bob was okay.

Both Bob and I were frustrated but for entirely different reasons. Bob's clothes were soaked, and he was cold. He wanted to leave the canyon, walk to the car, and drive home, while I felt we had just arrived and wanted to continue fishing. Not feeling empathetic toward Bob's predicament, I yelled asking him if he was okay. He nodded so I told him I was going to continue fishing, and he should wait on the shore until I eventually waded back across the river.

I was hit with the same question I asked myself in Montana. What should I do: leave the river or continue to fish? I probably should have been more sympathetic, but I rationalized that it was Bob's problem. He had not heeded my warning about wading carefully. Perhaps, Bob had tried to emulate me while watching me wade cross the river successfully.

I did my best to concentrate on fishing but after another forty-five minutes, I couldn't help noticing Bob sitting and shivering with his woeful head hanging down on the opposite bank. So begrudgingly, I finally gave in, waded back across the river, walked out of the canyon, and we left in my car for home. It was especially tough for me to justify driving over an hour to the river and only having a short time to fish.

A few weeks later, I related my story to two young avid fly fishermen named Jim and Klaus who were friends of my son, Writer. Jim fished as much as possible and had both of his legs fully tattooed with rainbow and German brown trout. Both guys stated emphatically that they would have fished even longer and felt no guilt. As they reiterated, it wasn't my fault that Bob got wet while wading in the river. These two serious fishermen certainly justified my position.

In hindsight, maybe I needed to view this happening differently. If you have never waded in a river, it can be treacherous and difficult. Could I expect Bob, who had no wading experience to stay out of trouble? If the situation was reversed, and I was cold and wet, I probably would have wanted to go home. How would you have handled this situation? Little did I know that a couple of similar wading experiences would befall me just a few years later.

Bob learned to be a competent wader and fly fisherman and primarily fished nymphs. Bob would rig his weighted leader with as many as three or four tiny imitation nymphs at one time. Occasionally when releasing a trout, he might hook one of his fingers with a fly or create a major tangle in his leader. Eventually, he learned to hook a few trout using a dry fly and a dropper.

Bob reminded me of a new breed of yuppy fly fisherman. He had his fishing vest heavily loaded with every conceivable gadget he could carry to enhance his experience. Over the years, I personally have lightened my own load and only carry the most necessary items. When fishing small streams, I wear a lanyard around my neck equipped with clippers, tippet, floatant, and tweezers while keeping a fly box in my shirt pocket. My mantra is "keep it light and simple."

Bob and I fished together several other times. Ironically, when I was ready to go home, he wanted to stay and fish even longer. Here's to my good friend, Bob, who could no longer be called "the tenderfoot."

Next: **Trip of a Lifetime**

CoolClips.com

# Chapter 7

# Trip of a Lifetime

---

*"Thrashing out of the water,*

*I began running down the riverbank*

*pursuing the king salmon.*

*I realized my only hope of landing*

*such a huge fish depended solely on*

*whether or not it stripped all my fly line*

*and backing from my reel*

*and snapped off my fly."*

---

61

In the early spring of 1979, my best friend Jim and I were talking about taking another fishing trip. The real estate market was hot, and the penny stock market was booming. Financially, we were making good money. Since Jim had made a previous trip to Alaska with his cousin to hunt caribou fourteen years earlier, he persuaded me to consider a trip so we could fly fish for trophy rainbow trout and salmon. This would be a special adventure trip.

Jim told me about a wild game and fish dinner hosted by a Denver taxidermy business named Jonas Brothers and called to find out if there would be any Alaskan fishing guides in attendance. The answer was yes, and a guide named Bill Sims would be attending. Jim made reservations and asked for us to be seated at Sim's table.

At the event, we hit it off with Sims who told us that he had been an Alaskan hunting guide until this past year. He was set up and arrested by Federal agents disguised as German hunters who paid him to guide them to kill a brown/grizzly bear. Sims had previously shot a caribou and left it to rot on the tundra to lure a bear to find the carcass. Sure enough, Sims' plan worked to perfection. He piloted his airplane with the hunters and noticed a bear feasting on the dead carcass. Sims landed on a lake nearby, led the hunters toward the dead caribou, spotted the bear, and one of his clients shot it. Sims was being paid handsomely, $20,000 for the brown bear.

Being an outlaw, Sims didn't care about the rules and regulations when so much money was at stake. Obviously, he was greedy one too many times, and the Feds, who were undercover as his clients, caught him red-handed. Paying dearly for using the baited-bear tactic, Sims told us he lost his Alaskan guiding and hunting permit for life, had his Cessna float plane confiscated, was fined $75,000, and served a jail term of 45 days. To say the least, he experienced a very painful and expensive lesson.

Sims had only one choice left to earn money. He would turn his hunting lodge into a desirable destination for sport fishermen. He was just beginning the process of booking fishermen for the upcoming summer season. Jim and I talked to Sims about joining him at his lodge for a week in mid-July and started negotiations regarding the price for a week's guided daily fly-out fishing trips for two.

After looking at other Alaskan fishing lodge's brochures and the high cost for a week's stay, we realized Sims' price of $900 for each of us was a bargain and accepted his offer. Even though Sims had no experience guiding fishermen, Jim and I figured we could catch fish if he could fly us to some promising rivers. We paid Sims a deposit for our July week and couldn't wait to take our trip to Alaska and catch trophy-sized rainbows and sockeye salmon. Our dream trip was quickly becoming a reality.

As Jim and I boarded the Alaskan Airlines flight to Seattle and Anchorage, we couldn't help but feel uneasy wondering if our rods and gear would make the flight after the Frontier Airlines debacles. Thankfully, everything arrived in Alaska without a hitch. After spending a night at a motel in Anchorage, we boarded a small Wien Airlines turboprop and landed after an hour flight on a short runway at Iliamna. It was a small hamlet located adjacent to Lake Iliamna in southwestern Alaska near the Aleutian Mountain range and not too far from the Bering Sea. During our flight, I was awestruck by the vastness and rugged beauty of the snowcapped majestic mountains and glaciers. Most of the countryside included miles and miles of tundra and water, and the pine trees were small and stunted because of the harsh winters and short growing season.

Upon our arrival, a bearded man walked up and introduced himself as Denny Thompson. Jim kept looking at Thompson and finally asked him if he might be the same person who guided he and his cousin on a caribou hunt over 10 years ago. Thompson perked up and said he did remember guiding them. What an amazing coincidence this turned out to be. Everything seemed to be falling right into place for us.

Jim and I loaded our rods and gear in Thompson's small Super Cub plane with only two seats. I had to kneel in the back for the short 20-minute flight to Sim's Newhalen Lodge on Lake Clark. As we flew low over the lake, Thompson pointed out the huge reddish-purple sockeye salmon population. It was the biggest salmon run in many years. While kneeling in the back of the plane, I had a good view out a rear window, and it was hard to comprehend this mass of reddish color was comprised of thousands of salmon.

Thompson made a bumpy landing on a short dirt strip behind the lodge. It was situated right on the water with two other Cessna float planes parked out front and just a short distance from a small local indigenous Indian village. Once settled in our room, we met Sims who told us there was one other party comprised of four fishermen booked during this same week. Sims would guide them while Thompson would take care of us. We figured that the other fishermen were paying a higher price for this same week, and Sims decided to guide them.

Jim and I were excited to have Thompson as our guide even though he told us he had no experience guiding fishermen. He would fly us to some of the same places he took hunters since there were rivers nearby. The fact that Thompson was not a fishing guide did not dampen our enthusiasm because we were sure every day would bring a new adventure for all three of us.

Later that afternoon, Thompson drove us in a motorboat across Lake Clark to fish near a river that flowed out of the lake. Arriving at our destination, we could hardly believe our eyes at all the tailing sockeye salmon. It didn't take long for Jim to hook a four or five pound one on a bright orange egg pattern, and this salmon took off across the lake toward the lodge like a freight train. There was no stopping this fish, and Jim's fly reel screeched as the line rapidly stripped off it into his backing. Jim and I were overmatched fishing our lightweight Orvis 6 foot, 6 weight graphite fly rods.

To slow this fish, Jim attempted to put extra pressure on the handle of his Hardy Princess fly reel by using his right palm and thumb which eventually caused his reel to seize up as the interior spool bent slightly. Jim had no chance to stop this salmon's run, and it quickly snapped off his fly. We were both amazed at the unrelenting power of these fish. Jim's right hand was bruised and painful, and his fly reel no longer operated. Fortunately, he had brought an extra spool filled with fly line. Jim knew it was time to make a change and fish his spinning rod and reel with heavier fourteen-pound test line instead.

In the meantime, it didn't take long for me to hook a salmon on my fly rod, and its power quickly tore off my fly. I followed Jim's reasoning and started casting my spinning rod. Our adrenalin was flowing as Jim and I both hooked and fought salmon after salmon. These fish would run one way, change directions, jump, twist, and fight as hard as any fish we had ever encountered. We were both exhausted after hooking and landing several sockeyes. Jim and I could not imagine a better beginning to our Alaskan fishing trip!

Our arrival coincided with the summer solstice in July where it stays light almost all night long. It isn't quite as bright as normal daylight, but you can see quite well. We could fish at night if Thompson was willing to guide us. The fishing conditions were especially good since most of the rivers were running lower than normal due to a drought. And best of all, the mosquitoes and black flies were not too bad either. This particular year, we chose the prime time to fish Alaska.

After breakfast the second morning, we took off in the Super Cub. There was an extra Cessna float plane available, but Thompson thought we would enjoy the scenery more with some low altitude flying. Due to space restrictions,

Jim had a window seat next to Thompson, and I knelt in back for the hour flight over and would switch positions for the flight back to the lodge.

Talk about flying close to the deck, Thompson skimmed at low altitude over the hills at about 60 or 70 miles per hour. It was perfect for viewing wildlife and waterfowl. He spotted and circled a large herd of caribou on the side of a big hill. We watched as a large brown bear stalked them and looked for an opportunity to make a rush to kill an unhealthy, older, or younger caribou. It was surprising the caribou would let the bear get so close while the herd congregated around the last remnants of a snowfield. Thompson told us the caribou liked to stand in the cold snow as it offered a respite from the annoying black flies.

As I tend to get motion sick, it wasn't long before my stomach began to feel queasy. What played a major part in my feeling nauseated was the fact that Thompson smoked a cigar in the pilot's seat directly in front of me. I couldn't help breathing the smoke wafting behind him.

After flying for an hour or so, Thompson pointed out the Nushagak River in the valley straight ahead. I hoped to make it to the river without vomiting, but during our final approach toward a short sandbar next to the river, I let go in a plastic garbage bag. The only saving grace was that

Thompson skillfully landed the plane on a sandbar not more than a hundred yards in length. He parked next to a smaller and shallower tributary of the main channel of the Nushagak River which was nearby and much wider and deeper.

After drinking some cola to settle my stomach and alleviating the unpleasant taste in my mouth, Jim and I put on our waders and vests, set up our Orvis fly rods, and tied on large, weighted black muddler minnow streamer flies. A little air sickness was not going to curtail my enthusiasm.

Deciding to fish a short way upstream where a smaller tributary entered the river, I made several casts where the two streams met and stripped my line back slowly. Within the first fifteen minutes or less, I felt a strong strike and was battling a large rainbow trout that jumped and fought like no other trout I had caught before. This big fish made run after run stripping line off my reel and taxing my lightweight Orvis rod. Luckily, this fish was in a slow narrow channel of the river. Otherwise, it is doubtful I could have landed it. After a long struggle, I netted this trophy-sized rainbow with a colorful dark green body and a bright red stripe down its sides. This trout was much longer than my net.

Due to short summers and long harsh winters, Alaskan trout grow slowly. This fish was an older specimen since it measured 27 inches long, and Jim and I estimated its weight at closer to five or six pounds. After the long strenuous struggle, it took me several minutes to revive the exhausted trout by moving it back and forth in the current so it could live to fight again. It was my first trout in Alaska and the largest rainbow I had ever caught so our trip was already a major success!

Let's face it, many fishermen are notorious for exaggerating the size and weight of their fish as it feeds their egos and makes their stories sound better. In the past, I remember thinking a trout was significantly longer or larger, but how much smaller the fish looked as I held it proudly in a photo. This rainbow was exceptionally large. I was higher than a kite. Spending the rest of the day fishing that same tributary, Jim and I caught a few other good-sized rainbows around twenty inches, but nothing could compare to my first fish.

A few minutes before we were ready to leave for the lodge, I cast to a similar spot where the tributary fed into the river. I was shocked back into reality as I felt a tremendous jolt and saw the wake of an enormous dark reddish colored fish as it swam straight at me. Stripping my fly line in as fast as possible to try to keep tension on this fish, it was obvious to me that I had no chance of stopping this monster's run. The battle lasted only a few seconds as the fish turned downstream and moved like a charging bull jerking its head and snapping off my fly. Sitting down on the bank, I was speechless. I replayed in my mind what had just happened as it was such an amazing sight. Thompson walked over and told me I had hooked a large king salmon, probably in the range of fifteen to twenty pounds.

When previously reading about fishing Alaska, both Jim and I had heard about king salmon, but had never given any thought to hooking one on a fly rod. These salmon were too big and strong and far beyond the capabilities of our rods. However, this moment still whetted our appetites to the possibility of hooking another king during our stay. The plane flight home was uneventful as Jim, and I daydreamed about catching more large fish on the Nushagak River. For sure, our fires were really lit!

Complying with our request to fish the same river the next day, Thompson piloted us in a Cessna float plane. It was special to fly in a much faster and roomier plane after our previous flight in the cramped Super Cub. He expertly set the Cessna down on the middle of the Nushagak River, and taxied to a sandbar not far from where the river made a left-hand bend. The weather was warm and beautiful, and the river was low, cold, and clear. Jim and I began wading and casting our fly rods directly in front of the plane. Stationing ourselves about thirty feet apart, we started catching fish, sometimes at the same time.

The most exciting aspect of fishing Alaska was that Jim and I never knew what species of fish we might catch next. One time it might be a rainbow while another time an arctic grayling, a dolly Varden, or a king salmon. The grayling is a silvery fish with a tall sharp dorsal fin and measures about ten to fifteen inches. These fish are not picky and will readily take most dry flies on the surface. The dolly is more colorful and resembles a brook trout but is larger.

Jim and I were both euphoric and couldn't stop laughing about our good luck. Amazingly, all our success was happening with a hunting guide who could offer no fishing advice. We were living an adventure that other fishermen could only dream about.

While standing in the clear river, my breathing rapidly increased as I spotted several huge, reddish-colored king salmon cruising upriver just a few feet in front of me. I yelled at Jim and pointed toward the salmon. Thinking how I might attract one of these giant fish to grab my fly, I decided to tie on a size #8 orange Wulff imitation that I had tied specifically for this trip. Instead of fishing the fly on the surface, I added a split shot to my leader sinking it deeper into the heavy current. I hoped my fly might attract a king to strike because it was colored more like an egg pattern.

Soon I felt a strong jerk, and a king salmon grabbed my fly and headed downstream. My rod vibrated, and my reel screeched as the line shot off it as this majestic fish jumped several times. Thrashing out of the river, I began running as quickly as I could down the riverbank. My only hope to land such a huge fish depended solely on whether I could keep it from snapping off my fly. Suddenly with a jerk of the king's head, my line went slack, and my orange Wulff was gone. Once this fish took off, I had no chance I could stop it.

Talking over lunch about the remote possibility of landing a king, Thompson mentioned that he had a rubber boat with a small outboard motor stowed in the cargo area of the airplane. With this amphibious craft, we could chase any hooked king salmon up or down the river increasing our odds of winning the battle. Thompson unloaded the rubber boat, used an air compressor to blow it up and attached the motor. Jim decided to use his spinning rod and reel with fourteen-pound line while I continued fishing my fly rod. With the boat ready for action, it was time to see if one of us could hook another king.

It wasn't long before an enormous king grabbed Jim's lure and took off jumping several times as it raced downstream. All three of us quickly climbed into the boat as the mono line peeled off Jim's open-faced Garcia reel. This giant fish made several jumps until it suddenly stopped moving. Jim's reeled in his slack line with no resistance as our boat approached the king's last known location in the deepest part of the river. He figured this salmon may have thrown his lure, but as the tension on his reel increased, he thought he might be snagged on a log at the bottom of the river. Thompson said he had heard a story about a king salmon that stopped in the middle of river and sulked. As Jim continued to firmly apply pressure, the king suddenly took off, and the battle continued. Jim and I took turns fighting this giant. After an epic struggle of twenty minutes or more, we beached the raft on a sandbar in slower and shallower water. Both of us waded into the river and pulled this huge king salmon onto the shore. There was no way to weigh it so we could only guess at its size. Denny thought this fish weighed between thirty or forty pounds. Jim and I took a photo before we slid the goliath back into the river. It slowly swam off to continue upriver to its spawning beds. Our trip just got much better!

After our success, I also decided to use my spinning rod, hooked another king, and chased it in the boat winning another battle. This fish fought fiercely, but was smaller, in the fifteen-to-twenty-pound range. Thompson decided to keep this salmon to be filleted for dinner.

It was time to leave for the lodge, but neither Jim nor I wanted to end our day. Flying back in silence, Thompson pointed out the Cessna's fuel gauge which showed almost empty. He thought there was enough fuel to reach the lodge but decided to follow the river below just in case the engine shut down, and he needed to land the plane on water. The possible fuel shortage made Jim and I uneasy, but the engine never sputtered until our final approach into Lake Clark. He landed the plane on the lake without a hitch, and as we pulled up to the lodge, the engine quit. Somebody was certainly looking after us. Jim and I wanted to savor this day forever!

We walked into the lodge and figured our day was over. After a delicious dinner, Thompson stopped by our room and asked if we would like to fly tonight to a nearby lake where he heard there might be some exceptional arctic char fishing. The char is related to the dolly but is a larger silvery species. Jim and I didn't hesitate to chorus yes and couldn't believe our good fortune.

Both of us felt a new burst of energy as we boarded the Super Cub, flew approximately twenty minutes to the lake, and made a soft bouncy landing on a plateau covered with tundra. Jim and I quickly rigged up our fly rods and tied on size #6 weighted black muddler minnow streamer flies.

While wading shallow water approximately twenty yards into the lake, we stood within thirty feet of each other making long casts, sinking our flies for a few seconds, and stripping our lines back toward us. It was just a short time before Jim and I both felt strikes within five minutes of each other. Laughing out loud and praising our good luck, we both fought artic char that made long runs forcing us to crisscross each other while keeping our lines from tangling together. It took us about ten minutes to each land a two-to-three-pound silvery char. Thompson yelled at us to keep these fish as the cook would serve them for another dinner. Our fishing success continued as we caught two more smaller char.

The evening sky was clear and almost as bright as daylight. While viewing the lake from a bluff above us, Thompson spotted a sockeye salmon concentration along another shoreline. Jim and I hiked down to find the best position to cast our spinning rods to these fish. We both hooked and fought several sockeyes before it was time to fly back to the lodge near midnight.

Landing those artic char on our fly rods provided the perfect ending to a phenomenal day and night of fishing in Alaska! So far, two days and three plane flights while catching many species of wild fish was more than Jim and I could ever imagine. We couldn't help pinching ourselves.

The rest of the week, our fishing was good, but nothing could compare to the first three days. No matter what flies we chose to present to these game fish, the action was phenomenal, especially on the Nushagak River. Jim and I were living the ultimate Alaskan fly-fishing adventure, the "trip of a lifetime."

Next: **Up to My Neck**

Keep your head above water

# Chapter 8

# Up to My Neck

---

"Not having any time to worry
or watch my life pass in front of me,
I was wet and cold, and knew
I had to reach shallow water
as soon as possible, or I might drown."

---

Jim and I made two more trips back to Alaska during the next three years. Since we were both making good money selling real estate, it was easy to justify the additional cost for each trip.

Jim and I were now totally immersed in Alaskan fishing and wanted to recreate our first trip by booking again with Sims for the following year in September. We brought along two friends, Ken, and Sandy, to join us. Sandy loved fly fishing while Ken was making the trip more for the adventure and camaraderie because he was not a fisherman.

After arriving at the Newhalen Lodge in late September, Jim and I inquired about our previous guide, Denny Thompson, but since Sims had lost his hunting guide permit, Thompson decided to leave for Africa and higher paying jobs guiding big game hunters. Recently, Sims had heard from him. Thompson and a friend were flying their planes at low altitude over South Africa when his friend's plane was shot down by militants. Luckily, Thompson's plane avoided any damage, but unfortunately, his friend was killed. Jim and I were relieved to hear he was okay.

On this fishing trip, Sims was going to be our exclusive pilot and guide. We would be fishing primarily for rainbow trout. The four of us were the only fishermen booked at the Newhalen Lodge. There was a hunting guide and two big game hunters from Mexico also staying there. Sim's friend, Ron Hayes, was guiding the hunters, a father and son on daily hunts. The Alaskan hunting regulations allowed the guide and his hunters to fly and spot an animal from an airplane. The restrictions required that the guide land his plane in the general area, camp overnight, and then guide his hunters to find, stalk, and shoot the wild animal during the next day.

While at the lodge, the hunters successfully shot several moose, caribou, and a brown bear all for the hefty fee of $50,000. Chatting with the hunters, we found out that they shot the animals on the same day that Hayes spotted them from the air. They killed a caribou in the morning and a moose during the same afternoon. These short hunts took the sporting aspect out of finding and stalking the animals the next day. Hayes was being greedy just like Sims and didn't care if he was breaking the law. Dollar signs were clouding Hayes' judgement because of the goldmine he had in his midst. Obviously, he had not learned a thing from Sim's previous costly lesson.

What we didn't find out until talking to Sims a year later was that these two Mexican hunters were also Federal agents who had booked this hunting trip over a year in advance. Just like Sims, Hayes was caught red-handed, found guilty, lost his guiding and hunting permit for life, a Cessna airplane, and was fined $150,000. Instead of jail time, he agreed to do community service and made a public service documentary movie for National Geographic about his illegal hunting activities.

Even Sims, who had been caught two years earlier by Federal agents posing as German hunters, had no idea the same thing was happening to his friend, Hayes, right in front of his eyes. The possibility of making easy, big money made both Sims and Hayes incriminate themselves. It was poetic justice that both men got exactly what they deserved for breaking the law.

Several years later, I was watching a National Geographic show and guess who appeared bigger than life? Here was Hayes telling his story and educating the public about his illegal hunting activities. Both Hayes and Sims were outlaws and until they ran afoul of the law, they felt untouchable!

I recently saw a story on the internet about Sims' son, Fred, who was also indicted by a grand jury in 2012 for baiting four brown/grizzly bears by killing moose. There was no information about how his case was resolved. However, it did seem like father, like son.

On our second trip, Sims flew all four of us to the Alagnak River. Jim and I started wading and fishing in a relatively straight stretch of the river. When we looked downstream where the river curved around a bend to the left, Ken was wading deeper and deeper. Jim and I were worried about him as he had no wading experience. Ken kept moving farther into the river, and the water was soon lapping around his chest. Having a difficult time keeping his balance while tiptoeing, bobbing, and swaying in the heavy current. Jim and I were both alarmed watching Ken struggle to keep his balance. Fortunately, he made his way back into shallower water. Jim and I were glad he was able to get out of trouble.

After extracting himself from the river, Ken walked back upstream to join us. Since it was a cool day, and his clothes were soaked from water pouring over the top of his waders, Ken asked if either of us had brought an extra set of dry clothes that he could borrow. I had extra clothes stored in the plane, so I gladly offered mine. After all, I knew I was an expert wader, and the same thing couldn't possibly happen to me. What do you think happened next? Little did I know that there was another big lesson awaiting me!

Not much more than an hour or so later, Jim and I found ourselves wading in approximately the same location where Ken had found himself in trouble. We had not learned a thing while watching his precarious situation. Wading deeper and deeper into the heavy current, Jim and I held onto each other's arms to keep our balance. I don't remember what we were thinking, but like Ken, we were putting ourselves at risk. Soon our wading boots were barely touching the bottom of the river, so we tiptoed trying to keep our balance. Jim suddenly let go of me and stumbled back into shallower water. I was not so lucky as he pushed me deeper into the river. I lost my balance and suddenly found myself immersed up to my neck. Thankfully, I had tightened a belt around my chest. Holding onto my rod with my left hand while dog paddling with my right, I floated downriver in the fast, cold water. Not having any time to worry or watch my life pass in front of me, I knew I had to get to shallower water as soon as possible. The current swung me around a left-hand turn and carried me several hundred feet toward the river's right shoreline where I finally felt my boots brush the bottom. Jim had quickly waded out of the river and saw my dangerous predicament. He ran down the bank and helped me struggle onto the rocky shore.

Later, I was cold and shivered in my wet and soggy clothing during what seemed like an interminably long one-hour plane flight back to the lodge while watching my friend Ken sitting in front of me as warm as toast wearing my dry clothes. How ironic it was for me as I remembered Bob's problem while wading the South Platte River. If only Jim and I had paid closer attention to Ken's near mishap. The last laugh was on me. I will always remember that day, September 17th as it is the same date as my wife's birthday. I was lucky to have escaped such a close call.

During this Alaskan trip with Ken and Sandy, the fishing was good. Sims flew us to new locations recommended by other fishing guides, but we never fished the Nushagak River. Sandy caught the most fish.

Our third and last trip to Alaska included two other friends, Fred, and Ron. This trip was also in September, but we stayed at a different lodge on a new lake and fished several different rivers. Ron had the most success catching rainbow trout and silver salmon using a spinning rod. We enjoyed all three trips with good fishing, but nothing could compare with our first one! I never again wanted to find myself "up to my neck."

Next: **Stalking a Rise**

# Chapter 9

# Stalking a Rise

---

*"Nothing can compare*
*with the satisfaction derived*
*from carefully casting a fly*
*to a waiting trout and*
*watching the fish rise and take it."*

---

D uring May 1984, there was another opportunity for Jim and I to return to Montana. On this trip we joined Fred and Ron from our third Alaskan trip. Ron was a pilot and flew us in a Cessna airplane from Denver nonstop to Fort Smith, Montana for a two-day float trip down the Bighorn River below Yellowtail Dam. It was early May, and we were hoping for good spring fishing.

Upon our arrival, our fishing guide nicknamed "Grizz" met us and drove us in his pickup truck to his lodge. He was quite a character, six feet two inches tall, heavy-set with long hair and a round face covered by a heavy unruly beard. "Grizz" told us he was part American Indian, spoke in a loud voice, laughed a lot, and loved to tell stories.

Unfortunately, there had been heavy rains during the past few days, and the Bighorn River was running muddy. During our first day on the river, Jim and I were fishing in a McKenzie drift boat with "Grizz" while Fred and Ron rode with another guide. Floating the upper ten-mile stretch of the river each day, "Grizz" suggested a deeper wet-fly fishing method using weighted streamers and slow stripping retrieves which netted us a few trout. Considering the murkiness of the water, Jim and I looked at the bright side since we both caught more fish than the other guys.

*Hooked by Fly Fishing.*                    Graham M. Mott

On the second day, the river was not quite so discolored and started clearing slightly so the catching prospects looked more promising. While on our morning float, we continued fishing the deep streamer method. By midday, "Grizz" pointed out to us that the river was beginning to clear up especially close to the banks. When we stopped for a shore lunch, Jim and I were frustrated after casting and retrieving our flies and not having much success. Both of us had caught one fifteen-to-eighteen-inch brown trout but never saw any fish rising on the river.

By late afternoon, "Grizz" decided to offer me a challenge since I had caught the most trout. Spotting a rising trout in shallow water near the bank ahead, he suggested I attempt to stalk and catch it. This trout was the only actively feeding fish we had seen all day. I was anxious to test my ability even though I wasn't sure I could make a proper cast without scaring or putting this fish down. A soft presentation of my dry fly was crucial.

"Grizz" beached the boat several hundred feet downstream of the rising trout. I attached my favorite dry fly, a size 16 Adams, exited the boat, and walked slowly down the bank staying twenty to thirty feet away from the shore. Moving as stealthily as possible toward the place where the fish was actively feeding, I crouched down and moved on my hands and knees crawling slowly so I would not spook it. Staying closer to the river, I could readily view the trout rhythmically rising. I made a couple of false casts on shore attempting to gauge the correct length of line needed to make the proper cast. I would probably have only one opportunity to hook this trout. After crawling within twenty feet of the fish, I viewed it continuing to rise and sip a bug every few seconds. From what I could see, it looked like it might be a good-sized trout.

There is a defining moment every fly fisherman lives for: entice the trout to take his fly. Slowing my breathing pattern down, it seemed as if time was standing still. Sitting on my knees, I held my breath as I slowly raised my Orvis rod and cast my parachute Adams above the waiting prize. Watching intently as the fly landed softly on the surface of the river and floated slowly downstream, suddenly the shallow water exploded as the trout seized it with a vengeance. Raising my rod and standing up, I yelled loudly in triumph as the fish made a run into deeper, faster water. Fighting this trout was enjoyable but nothing could compare to stalking it and making the perfect cast. I netted my prize, a beautifully colored seventeen-inch German brown trout. Jim and "Grizz" congratulated me on my success. Of course,

I felt like a million dollars since I had successfully completed "Grizz's" challenge.

Over the years, I had become a competent dry fly fisherman, but there were times when my poor casting had frightened a rising fish. I am not particularly stealthy, but on this occasion, I had been extra careful during my approach and made a superb presentation. Everything had worked out perfectly, and the moment was all mine. "Grizz" repeated my success story to the other fishermen who joined us for dinner, and I couldn't keep from beaming.

This fishing trip fell far short of our expectations due to the murky water conditions. For two full days of fishing, each of us only averaged catching less than five trout per day. It was an expensive trip weighed against the number of fish caught, but any time you make plans to travel to fish a distant location, you cannot control the weather or river conditions. This seemed to be a moot point when put in perspective to our overall experience. The flying was fun, the camaraderie good, and the scenery beautiful.

Several years later, my son, Writer, and I took two other trips to Montana. One was to fly fish the Big Horn and the other, the Missouri River. During the latter, Writer developed pink eye, and we had to drive to a clinic in Missoula to get medication. We just missed the caddis fly hatch on the Missouri, but during our float trips on both rivers, we caught several trout.

One thing for sure, I would never forget my magical moment on the Big Horn River. Here is to you, "Grizz," for offering me the challenge of "stalking a rise."

Next: **Double Jeopardy**

# Chapter 10

# Double Jeopardy

---

*"In your wildest dreams,*

*no one could think up*

*such a farfetched happening.*

*It was beyond anyone's comprehension."*

---

In 1986, I remember attending Boy Scout camp for two nights with my son, Writer and stepson, J.D., as a volunteer chaperone to help Allan, the Scout Master. Each scout troop was required to have at least two adults always present in camp. My boys' scouting experience consisted of a one week stay in mid-July at a camp located among rolling hills and ponderosa pine trees east of Denver near Elizabeth, Colorado.

My son, Writer, aged twelve, had heard the rumor that there were large rainbow trout in the small lake used for life-saving and canoeing classes. He was an avid spin fisherman so we both packed our rods and gear hoping to have the opportunity to fish one afternoon. I communicated this information to Allan, and his son, Doug, who also loved to fish.

During the second afternoon after the regular camp activities had ceased, Allan, Doug, J.D., Writer, and I arrived at the lake. Dinner was scheduled at 6:30pm, so we only had a short fishing window.

This man-made lake was more like a large pond located in the open with a dam at one end and a few bushes and trees around it. We spotted an occasional fish rising within casting distance of the shore. It was a beautiful, partly cloudy day with a slight breeze. I was using my Orvis fly rod while Writer cast his spinning rod using a large #7 chartreuse Rapala lure with two sets of treble hooks. Personally, I never liked this type of lure because the multiple hooks could be dangerous. I had no idea how prophetic my thoughts would turn out to be! Can you guess what might be coming?

It didn't take long for both Allan and I to hook a rainbow trout. Both fish were heavy and measured approximately eighteen-to-twenty-inches. I was sure there must be freshwater shrimp in the lake which quickly fattened up these trout. Writer hooked the largest fish of the day. This rainbow trout jumped several times, made long runs, and fought hard. Having honed his fishing skills as a member of the Junior Bass Masters' Club, Writer was exceptionally good at catching bass, crappie, and blue gill. Having 10-pound test on his reel, he finally horsed this 22-inch rainbow up onto the shore where it flopped about wildly.

Trying to be the dutiful Dad, I told Writer I would remove the lure from the trout. What a mistake I was about to make! As I bent over the fish and placed my left hand on its slimy body, I attempted to remove the Rapala lure with my right hand. Suddenly, the trout thrashed wildly, threw the lure out of its mouth, and somehow it landed directly in my right hand sinking one of the treble hook's barbs deeply into my palm. At the same time, the fish flipped back into the lake and was gone. The Rapala was now dangling loosely from my palm, and there was no way I could remove it myself. To say the least, I was quite distressed and cussed loudly. Allan, Doug, Writer, and J.D. crowded around me to get a closer look at my predicament.

Luckily for me, Allan told me there was no problem removing this lure as he knew a quick method to extricate it from my palm. He said this process was like tying a piece of dental floss around a loose tooth and jerking it free. Naturally, I was game to try anything because I didn't want to leave camp and make the drive to a hospital emergency room.

First, Allan cut the line attached to the Rapala, and another three-foot length of mono line from Writer's reel. To be extra careful, he also removed the second set of treble hooks from the Rapala lure and was now ready to remove the it. I stood with my hands at my sides with my palms facing out. Placing the line around the shank or curve of the hook, Alan wrapped both ends around his wrist and quickly jerked in the opposite direction from which the hook had originally entered my palm.

This removal method worked flawlessly as the hook came loose painlessly. Now, try to guess what happened next? You won't believe it! There was just one major problem. After jerking the hook out of my right palm, the slack line made the lure swing freely in the air. Can you guess where this loose-flying object would land this time? The lure's one treble hook buried itself even more deeply in the palm of my left hand. What a calamity! How could a double hook-up be happening to me? It was unbelievable!

I was flabbergasted and loudly uttered more profanity laced words about my dilemma. No one could make up such a farfetched and farcical happening. I could not find any humor in this surreal moment, but Allan, Doug, J.D, and Writer all chuckled nervously at my new predicament. My only choice was to grin and bear it. Too bad this incident wasn't caught on film as it would have made one great fishing blooper.

Alan and I decided to be more careful with the second extraction. I placed my right hand behind my back, and Allan quickly jerked the lure loose from my left. This time the Rapala swung loosely and did not hook me or anyone else.

Overall, I was lucky that the hooks were stuck in the tougher skin of my palms. I didn't bleed much and healed quickly. Thankfully, Alan's hook extraction method saved me paying medical costs. I am not sure if I would have allowed him to remove the hook from my lower lip, but I do believe his method would have worked perfectly.

A few years later, Writer, who was night fishing at a lake near a power plant in Boulder, caught a large wiper, a hybrid stiped bass, which threw one of the treble hooks deeply into his index finger. The big problem for him was the fish was still hooked to the other treble hook, and every time the wiper struggled, the hook lodged itself more deeply in his finger. His friend, Klaus, came to his aid and grabbed the fish and unhooked it. Writer's finger was very painful, and he never considered letting me remove it. Instead, he drove to a nearby hospital's emergency room and had a doctor extract the hook.

A year or so later, Writer and I were fishing the Roaring Fork River near Aspen. While climbing out of the water, Writer tripped and deeply imbedded a size 16 parachute Adams in the fourth finger of his left hand. Using Allan's method, I quickly removed the hook, and we continued our fishing day. Over the years, I have successfully extracted several other hooks imbedded in friends and relatives.

My getting "hooked" reminded me of a story my mother told me when she was a teenager. She rode a train with her brother to fish a lake in Indiana. While fishing out of a rowboat, her brother cast his rod and stuck one of his lure's hooks in the top of her head. My mother was mortified on the train ride home with a large wooden lure nestled in her hair. After arriving, my grandfather, who was a doctor, removed it.

If you spend time fishing, there is no doubt you will stick a hook in your clothes or body. Remember, be especially careful when casting and always avoid "double jeopardy."

Next: **Portaging in Canada**

# Chapter 11

# Portaging in Canada

*"It was especially difficult for me*
*to wear a heavy cloth backpack*
*and balance a 90-pound canoe*
*over my head while walking*
*through mud, water, and trees."*

During my boys' membership in Boy Scouts, the Scoutmaster, Allan, suggested a week's summer trip to the Boundary Waters in Canada. Once again, I offered to go as a second adult chaperone on this excursion. It was not really a fly-fishing trip, but Writer and I were anxious to try our luck fishing for small mouth bass, northern pike, and walleye.

By the time J.D., Writer, and I were ready to leave for the Boundary Waters, our group numbered seven including two adults, three scouts and two friends. Our plane flight flew from Denver to Ely, Minnesota near the border of Canada. From there, we rode a bus to the Northern Tier Boy Scout camp situated on Moose Lake. It was only a short distance across the lake to a Canadian border outpost.

Our travel plans worked perfectly, and we arrived at the camp ready to start our week's exploration of Canada's lake country. Four of us would each carry canoes on portages going from one lake to the next. Each aluminum canoe weighed ninety pounds making it heavy and cumbersome to maneuver while holding it over our heads. We were issued cloth backpacks, two large four-man tents, and military C-ration packets for food.

Limited to how much weight each person could carry, I bought three cheap telescoping spinning rods with reels attached at the Army Surplus store. The fishing gear was poor quality, but we would make the best of it. In hindsight, I should have purchased compact fly-fishing rods, but my boys had not learned to fly fish yet.

The camp provided a young, friendly curly-haired volunteer named Franz to help guide us through the lake country. On the first day, we put our canoes in the water on Moose Lake and started rowing toward the other side. For most of us, it was our first-time learning how to row a canoe. When we arrived on the far side of the lake, four of us raised the 90-pound canoes over our heads balancing them precariously as we marched between trees to the Canadian border outpost. Our paperwork was quickly approved, and we crossed into Canada for the weeklong trip. Franz had carefully planned our route on his map to guide us through the various lakes and portages.

After canoeing partway across our second lake, we stopped to eat lunch and let the boys go for a swim. My stepson, J.D., decided to jump into the water and unfortunately, hit his knee against a rock. He had an open bloody gash which required some stitches to close the wound. J.D., who was the tallest boy, took one look at his injury and passed out.

This incident reminded me of a later story about J.D., who was 6'4" and attending a class in Construction Management at Colorado State University. While watching a movie on industrial injuries, he felt warm and passed out again. The professor found him lying on the classroom floor and had a good sense of humor announcing to the class that during the next semester, he would be adding seatbelts to every chair. It was obvious the sight of any blood made J.D. queasy.

Allan looked in his first aid kit and found some butterfly clips to keep J.D,'s wound knitted together. He disinfected the cut, wrapped his knee with gauze and tape, and used some sticks to keep his leg rigid and straight. During the rest of our excursion, J.D. had to be careful not to reopen his cut. His injury limited all his activities as he could no longer carry a backpack or a canoe. The rest of our group would take over J.D.'s tasks.

It was especially difficult for me to wear a heavy cloth backpack and balance a ninety-pound canoe over my head while trudging through mud, water, brush, and trees. From time to time, I couldn't help banging the front of my canoe against a tree vibrating my head and body. It was impossible to always keep the canoe in a stable position. Many times, I found these portages between lakes to be ultra-difficult. Our guide, Franz, while carrying his canoe, found himself sunk in mud up to his thighs and could not move until two of us helped free him from his predicament. At dusk each day, a large swarm mosquitoes appeared so we would run and climb into our tents and sleeping bags to avoid any bites. As the week progressed, my portaging skills improved but by the end, I was glad the trip was over. I felt as if I had accomplished an endurance test, and the military C-rations were barely edible and tasteless. Writer and I would have liked to have spent more time fishing the lakes in Canada, but we still managed to catch several small mouth bass.

My lesson was to always purchase quality fishing gear as our cheap spinning rods were not worth keeping by the end of our trip. Fly fishing would have been much more fun. Writer's friend, Derek, caught the only northern pike, and Allan landed a walleye. J.D.'s knee knitted together perfectly with only a small scar.

Our trip was a memorable adventure listening to the plaintive calls of the loons and enjoying the unmatched beauty and scenery of the Boundary Waters. I loved most of it except "portaging in Canada."

Next: **Dream Stream**

# Chapter 12

# Dream Stream

---

*"When I finally waded close enough to cast*
*a black weighted woolly booger*
*through the pool, I felt a heavy strike,*
*quickly raised my Winston rod and set the hook.*
*From the tension, I knew I had hooked a big trout."*

---

There was a time when Writer and I liked to fish Spinney Mountain Reservoir on opening day in the spring just after the temperatures were rising and the ice was gone. Annually, a large exodus of fishermen arrived to see if they could catch some fish. Everyone hoped the trout were hungry and active with the start of a new season.

Writer and I waded in the shallow water fishing close to shore. This day the catching was slow due to windy conditions creating waves on the lake. It was almost impossible to cast my fly rod, so I quit fishing and stood watching as Writer fished his spinning rod and a Rapala lure under the water. Suddenly, he felt a strike, and the struggle was on. Had Writer hooked a trout or another species? It wasn't long before we were both surprised as he reeled in a three-foot-long northern pike. A fisherman nearby asked if he could have the pike, so we gave it to him. Just a few minutes later, Writer hooked and landed another smaller pike. As far as I know, these were the first two pike that Writer caught in Colorado, and I have never had that experience.

Late in the summer a year later, I drove Writer, J.D., and a friend, Jeremy, to Spinney to fly fish the reservoir in float tubes. I made sure all three boys wore lifejackets. Jeremy borrowed my tube and fins. Soon, all three boys floated languidly on the lake hoping to hook some trout. They paddled slowly casting their flyrods and covered approximately one third of the lake's shoreline in a couple of hours. It was a beautiful sunny day, and I loved watching the boys having a good time. The fishing was slow, and Writer caught the only two trout.

The South Platte River flows in and out of Spinney. The outlet below includes a famous three-mile stretch of the meandering river with some excellent trout habitat. It is known as the Dream Stream between Spinney and Eleven Mile Reservoirs and is designated Gold Medal water requiring flies and lures only and catch and release regulations.

In the afternoon, the three boys and I tried our luck wading and fishing the river but did not have much success. It takes an experienced fly fisherman to catch trout on the Dream Stream. Jim and I had fished this stretch of the South Platte several times with only moderate success.

During the late fall, the river was known for large German brown trout that move up into the river from Eleven Mile Reservoir. One October day, Jim and I were fishing the Dream Stream when I approached a long run that narrowed into a deeper pool at one end. I finally waded close enough to cast a black weighted woolly booger deeply through the pool and felt a heavy strike, quickly raised my Winston rod, and set the hook. From the tension, I knew I had hooked a big trout. This fish made several runs back and forth until I was able to net it. I revived this brown trout by sliding it back and forth in the current until it took off down the river. I don't remember the exact size but would guess it was more than twenty inches and several pounds. This was the largest trout I ever caught on the "Dream Stream."

Next: **Mean Green**

# Chapter 13

# Mean Green

---

*"Looking down into the river,*
*it was almost like being*
*on top of a huge aquarium*
*where many fish swam beneath us*
*in the crystal-clear water,*
*and what a spectacle it was."*

---

I remember hearing stories from several other fisherman about catching trophy-sized trout during large insect hatches on the Green River in Utah. One acquaintance named Jodie, who was a teammate of mine on a local softball team, told me he regularly fished the river directly below Flaming Gorge Dam using a float tube. Jodie bragged about catching many large trout during the famous cicada hatch. He said float tubing the river was a piece of cake. His rhetoric caught my attention, and I decided to find out firsthand what this Green River buzz was all about.

I had recently purchased a new Winston 8'4", 4 weight, graphite fly rod which was now my favorite. It didn't take long for me to plan a trip with my boys, J.D, 16, and Writer, 15, and we would try our luck float tubing this stretch of the Green River below Flaming Gorge Dam. On the drive from Denver, we met my friend, Jim, at Trappers Lake in the Flattops Wilderness area near Rifle, Colorado. Trappers is a beautiful clear high-mountain lake surrounded by forest on all sides and home to mostly cutthroat trout and some brookies. It is catch and release on all cutthroats, but you could keep brook trout. The lake's water temperature was cold and since all of us had brought lightweight canvas chest waders rather than the newer and warmer neoprene type, our feet and legs cramped up during long floats on the lake. The problem while attempting to fish from shore was a cloud of mosquitoes waiting to attack so it was imperative to be out float tubing on the water. Everyone caught a few rising trout, but the action was far from fast and furious. Even in July, the evenings were crisp and cold in our tents. Sitting around a warm campfire, the camaraderie was great, and it was wonderful to get away from the daily grind.

J.D., Writer, and I only spent one evening at Trappers and the next day, we said goodbye to Jim, who was staying to fish the lake another day, and drove on to our next adventure at the Green River. None of us had float-tubed on a river before so we were rookies. I did bring life vests for all of us in case we got into any trouble. Neither J.D. nor Writer was an accomplished fly fishermen yet, but both knew how to cast a fly rod with some consistency. We were hoping for some superior dry fly fishing. Was I being naive to even attempt a float-tubing trip since none of us had knew this river?

Upon reaching the Flaming Gorge reservoir, which is a long, deep winding lake with high steep sides, we stopped at a tackle store to talk with the locals about the fishing conditions as well as the recommended fly-fishing techniques and best flies used to catch trout. I purchased several large cicada imitations and Utah two-day fishing licenses. Unfortunately, the cicada hatch was spotty now with only a few bugs on the water. This year's hatch cycle had been affected adversely by a prolonged period of high-water runoff. Our prospects for dry fly fishing did not look good.

On the drive to our campground, we stopped at a parking area on the Green River approximately seven miles below the dam and talked to a Utah Park Ranger. When I mentioned we were going to float-tube the river the next morning, he suggested maybe we should reconsider our plans. The Ranger mentioned that a couple of float-tubers had drown on this river in recent years and told us float-tubing was not a safe way to navigate the river due to several dangerous rapids. He thought it was just a matter of time before float-tubing on this upper stretch of the Green River would be restricted by the state of Utah. If we were going ahead with our plans, the Ranger recommended we exit the river when approaching any rapids and walk around the dangerous portions to avoid any potential trouble. He also suggested I might consider hiring a reputable fishing guide to float us down the river in his raft instead. After listening to the Ranger's warnings, I still didn't want to change our plans, nor did I want to spend the extra money for a guided raft trip. In retrospect, it would have been money well spent.

Thanking the Ranger for his advice, I assured him we would be extra careful float-tubing the river.

I drove to our campground where the boys and I set up our tents and ate dinner before the darkening skies surrounded us. As I talked to them about our plans before climbing into our sleeping bags, we all agreed that nothing was going to deter us from float-tubing down the river. However, we would heed the Ranger's warning by hiking around any rapids that might look difficult to maneuver.

The next morning, we parked our car seven miles downstream at the take-out spot and paid a tackle shop employee to ferry us in his truck back to the put-in area right below the dam. Located on the right side of the spillway, J.D, Writer and I set up our fly rods. Having previously filled our float tubes with air, we put on our waders, life vests and fins, grabbed our rods, climbed into our tubes, walked into the river, and pushed off from shore.

Looking down into the clear water, it was almost like being on top of a huge aquarium. We spotted a few large trout cruising beneath us. What a spectacle it was! J.D, Writer and I tried fishing weighted nymphs, but since we were not accomplished nymph fishermen, none of us had any success. We probably were fishing our flies at incorrect depths or not using the right pattern to attract a strike.

Watching in amazement, boatload after boatload of fisherman and rafters quickly passed by us. By contrast, we stayed close to the shore on one side and just relaxed and enjoyed our warm sunny day floating slowly and leisurely down the river.

Before lunch, J.D, Writer and I approached the first set of rapids. It was impossible for me to get the Ranger's warning out of my mind. Carefully looking at the fast-moving white water, I decided it was best to walk around the rapids. Each of us had brought an extra pair of sneakers so we climbed out of our tubes and put on our shoes. We carried our fly rods and placed the float-tubes over one shoulder. Just like portaging in Canada, it was an unwieldy, cumbersome, and awkward method traversing a narrow and meandering path up and down through trees and brush. After circumventing the first set of rapids, we were hot and sweaty. To keep hydrated, we stopped, drank water, and ate our lunches.

Then we launched our tubes and floated farther down the river. With rapids approaching more often, the same evasive procedures had to be followed at least four or five more times. Our fun day on the Green River had turned into a grueling test of endurance. Avoiding each set of rapids became more and more tedious and frustrating. The temperature in the canyon was hot, and it seemed as if our treks around each new rapid was more difficult and strenuous. As time passed, my frustration grew, and I couldn't help complaining about our plight.

By the time we skirted the last rapids and approached our take-out spot, it was almost 7pm. Our ordeal had become a grueling nightmare. What was to have been a fun day's floating and fishing had turned into a hellish experience, and to top it all off, the boys and I never caught one trout. I had witnessed only a handful of fish rise to the surface, and most were late in the day as we completed our ordeal. Still, I was glad I listened to the Ranger's warnings and had no regrets about maneuvering around each rapid. My boys and I had completed the seven-mile float-tubing trip in just over nine hours. Rafters could float this same stretch of river in less than a half day.

Sitting in our camp that night while smelling the aroma of burgers cooking on the grill, we could laugh about our long difficult day. We had accomplished our goal even though we never caught a trout. After the boys and I filled our stomachs with a delicious dinner, we quickly fell asleep.

The next morning, I finally hooked a small ten-inch German brown trout using a parachute Adams. By noon, we were ready to depart and make the five-hour drive back to

Denver. This was my first fly fishing trip with both my boys, and I cherished every minute of it. Float-tubing the Green River below the dam and hiking around the rapids was a unique experience none of us would ever forget. Looking back on this event, it didn't seem nearly as difficult a grind as it felt like at the time. Our trip only whetted my appetite to fish the Green River during the famous cicada hatch. If we returned, I would hire a knowledgeable fishing guide. Our unique float-tubing experience could only be dubbed the "Mean Green."

**Next: Mesmerized**

# Chapter 14

## Mesmerized

---

"Watching three young men with spinning rods

moving in below us to fish the deep pools,

it quickly became evident

that these fellows were fishing worms

and keeping trout on a stringer

violating the State of Colorado fishing regulations."

---

119

There was a time in the early 90s when Writer and I would drive up to the South Platte River by way of Sedalia and fish a stretch not far below Deckers, Colorado. At the time, Writer was in high school and working during the summer at the Discount Fishing Tackle store on south Santa Fe Dr. in Denver, CO. We would fish in the morning until he had to be back at work mid-afternoon. It was July, and there was always the possibility of finding a blue quill hatch.

I parked our car on a hill overlooking the river. When we looked downstream, it was wider, slower, and shallower with one big riffle and seam down the middle while upstream it narrowed into a canyon with large deep pools, big boulders and undercut banks. The South Platte River below Cheesman Reservoir was considered one of the best trout streams in the world based on the number of fish per mile and its proximity to Denver. It was a ninety-minute drive to reach the river from the city and was truly a remarkable trout fishery.

Writer and I were wading the river by 9am. Initially, the fishing was slow during the first hour, so we cast our parachute Adams hoping to raise some fish. It was a warm, partly cloudy day which usually was a good omen for dry fly action. I remember looking down the river several hundred yards where it came around a bend. What did I spot moving upriver but a cloud of blue quill flies. I yelled at Writer and pointed toward this large concentration of bugs. Being mesmerized by this amazing sight, we both knew the fishing activity would be picking up quickly. A few trout were already rising as the first insects arrived. I had seen hatches before but never witnessed one moving slowly upriver.

Writer and I both fished Adams in the narrower, deeper pools and caught several beautifully marked German brown trout. The hot action lasted for almost a half hour or so and then began to wane as the bugs moved upstream.

We decided to take a break and walked back uphill to our car while talking about this sizeable hatch and savoring the moment. Watching three young men with spinning rods moving in below us to fish the deep pools, it quickly became apparent that these fellows were fishing worms and keeping trout on a stringer violating the State of Colorado fishing regulations. There were signs posted along the road proclaiming flies and lures only and catch and release. The guilty fishermen's car was parked nearby with a sticker on the back window with the printed words, Ft. Carson, an army base located near Colorado Springs. We believed these men were soldiers stationed there. It was obvious they could care less about breaking the fishing rules.

Writer and I talked about this situation. There was nothing we could do to stop this activity as cell phones were not yet in service and no way to alert the Colorado Game and Fish Department to this illegal activity. Even if cell phone service had been available, apprehension would have been a long shot. What would you have done if faced with a similar situation?

Pointing downstream, I said to Writer, "Do you see that wider and shallower stretch of river? Let's walk down and see if we can catch some more trout." I thought this would provide a good lesson for Writer on reading and fishing different types of water. Situating Writer in what I thought looked like the best water on the left side, I fished the other. Noticing some trout rising in the shallows, he cast his fly while slowly wading upstream.

I spent more time watching Writer than fishing myself. He made an excellent cast softly landing his Adams near the bank. Suddenly, there was a big splash and wake in the shallow water as a trout moved quickly and gulped his Adams. It was a sizable rainbow that made several good leaps and runs back and forth across the river. Finally, after a good fight, I netted his fish. We both looked at this beautifully marked trout with red stripes down the side, and it measured seventeen inches long.

All the other fish we caught this day did not compare to this one. Carefully reviving his rainbow, Writer watched it swim away disappearing into the current. I knew he was surprised to catch such a large trout in shallow water and had learned a valuable lesson.

When we arrived back at our car, the soldiers were gone with their stringer of illegally caught trout. We did not let that incident dampen our good feelings. It was a spectacular day on the South Platte River with a large blue quill hatch providing plentiful dry fly-fishing action.

During the drive home, I reminisced about fishing with Writer's grandfather, Hal, at the Wigwam Club just a mile up the road. Writer and I also relived our remarkable fishing day when that cloud of flying insects slowly approached, and we were "mesmerized."

Next: **Phantom Canyon**

*Hooked by Fly Fishing.*                    Graham M. Mott

# Chapter 15

# Phantom Canyon

---

*"Our lack of fly-fishing success*
*made no difference*
*on this warm summer morning.*
*It was a watershed moment*
*where I could almost snap a photo*
*as a memory of this gorgeous location."*

---

There was a buzz among fly fishermen about a new stretch of pristine fishing water that had been purchased by the Nature Conservancy. It was a mile or two of the Cache La Poudre River on a ranch just 30 miles north of Fort Collins, Colorado along highway 287 toward Laramie, Wyoming and about one and a half hours from Denver. Supposedly, there had been no fishing pressure on this 170-acre property for years as it had been held privately as a ranch until the Nature Conservancy purchased the property so it could never be developed. The river was located at the bottom of a steep canyon.

It was necessary to make a phone reservation to fish the property as there were only four fly fishermen allowed each day to fish one of the four different sections or "reaches" of the Poudre River. There was minimal signage as I parked my car a short distance off the highway next to a cattle guard. A man picked us up and drove to a ranch house where we read the rules and regulations, signed an agreement, assembled our fishing gear, and made the steep hike into the canyon to reach the river below.

The first time, I took my stepson, J.D., to fish Phantom Canyon. Both of us would each fish our own private "reaches" of the river. We were warned to be careful walking down the to the river due to a prevalence of rattlesnakes in the area.

We hiked down the steep path into the bottom of the valley ahead. I started fishing below J.D. in the morning and would occasionally spot him in his "reach" ahead of me. For a river which had little fishing pressure with low, clear water conditions, I was surprised that I didn't see or move many trout. Not having many strikes, I did manage to catch one ten-inch German brown. Our lack of fishing success made no difference on this warm summer day. It was a watershed moment where I could almost snap a photo as a memory of this gorgeous location.

At lunchtime, I walked downstream and joined J.D., who had been shutout and decided to spend the afternoon watching him fish. I thought I could give him some pointers about fishing the river.

After eating lunch, we made a short, quick hike along the trail to the next fishing run. While walking in front of me and moving around a blind turn on the path, J.D. stopped suddenly and backed right into me. He said there was a rattlesnake on the path in front of us. Sure enough, the snake was coiled with its rattles vibrating. I suggested poking it with my flyrod to make it strike and move away, but J.D. didn't care for that idea. We watched the snake for a couple of minutes until it eventually slid off the path into the bushes. My previous history included encountering several rattlers growing up in the desert southwest, but for J.D., it was his first time seeing one in the wild. There was no doubt that his heart was beating faster than mine.

J.D. fished for another hour with no luck, so we decided to leave and make the steep hike out of the canyon. Overall, the fishing was poor, but the adventure was fun, and J.D. had his first face-to-face meeting with a Colorado rattlesnake.

During my second visit to Phantom Canyon the next summer, I included my son, Writer. This valley was such a special place to visit so I knew he would enjoy the experience. Again, we would be fishing adjoining "reaches" on the Poudre River. Just like my previous visit, the fishing action was slow. Writer caught one brown trout, and I hooked a couple but didn't land any.

During the afternoon, I joined Writer, and we fished together in his "reach." I was fishing a size #16 parachute Adams. While wading, I approached a steep bank where Writer was standing. Deciding to climb out of the river, I reeled in my line and attached my fly to the small wire loop or eyelet located in front of the handle on the bottom of my Winston fly rod. Most fly rods have this wire loop called the "tip top" to hook your fly to when not fishing. It keeps your fly hooked and line taut as you are walking.

As I reached for Writer's hand to help pull me up on the bank, I was holding the rod with my left hand and didn't realize that it was wrapped directly around the wire loop or eyelet where the fly was hooked to my rod. With Writer's help pulling me upward, I attempted to get up on the bank. I fell onto my knees putting my left hand holding the rod down on the ground and imbedded the parachute Adam's barb deeply into my left palm. Could this really be happening to me again? I was incredulous at my predicament. This crazy incident took only a few seconds before I realized what had occurred. The barb was stuck securely into my palm and attached to the wire loop or eyelet. My hand and the Adams were fastened directly to my fly rod. Believe it or not, my palm and fly rod were stuck tightly together. It was another comical moment, but I wasn't laughing. This was the third time I had a barbed hook stuck in one of my palms.

I said to Writer, "I am in real trouble. I can't believe it. I have hooked my left hand directly to my fly rod. How can this be happening to me?" I knew Allan's reliable fly removal method wouldn't work this time. Writer stared wide-eyed and disbelieving at my predicament. It was a weird happening. How could I remove the hook this time?

I figured there was only one way to solve my problem. Mustering my courage, I quickly ripped my left hand straight forward away from the rod, and the hook tore out of my palm. I checked my handiwork and only bled slightly. Thankfully, I had quickly alleviated another crazy hook-up.

By now, you probably think I am clumsy or accident prone, but when you fish often, it is just a matter of time before you hook yourself or someone else. I have fished many times since these humorous incidents and have never hooked myself again. Of course, this doesn't include the numerous occasions I snagged my hat, shirt, vest, net, boots, or laces.

The rest of the day in the canyon was uneventful. Writer and I never saw a rattlesnake during the steep hike in or out of the canyon, but another fisherman encountered one on the trail. The highlight of our fishing trip was that bizarre incident of hooking my palm directly to my fly rod. Fishing was slow, and Writer caught the only German brown trout. Keeping everything in perspective, nothing could mar our good feelings after another day at "Phantom Canyon."

Next: **Hit the Jackpot**

# Chapter 16

# Hit the Jackpot

---

*"At times, you could see large trout*
*cruising the shoreline, while at other times*
*you could cast a dry fly to rising fish.*
*We could not believe our good luck*
*as the fishing was so spectacular."*

---

For my birthday, my son, Writer, gave me another Winston fly rod. This was a three-piece, 8'4", 4 weight rod. Also included was a Ross reel with four-pound floating line. I loved this new rod as it fit in such a short compact case. I was a lucky father. Now, I had every Winston fly rod I could ever want.

One day, my best friend, Jim called me very excited and said he knew where there was some great fly fishing near his home in Evergreen, Colorado. He told me about two municipal ponds located near the Evergreen Recreation Center and Hiwan Golf Club. A fish stocking truck containing large-sized rainbow trout was travelling to the mountains and developed mechanical problems near Evergreen. It was a hot summer's day, and the trout were in distress so the fish needed to be unloaded as soon as possible. When the truck was operating, the company looked for a nearby location to dump the fish and chose the two closest Evergreen ponds.

Jim just happened to be driving by when he spotted the fish stocking truck unloading trout in the upper pond. He stopped and asked the truck driver what was happening? After hearing the news, he could hardly wait to grab his fly rod and start fishing. Could such an unexpected bonanza really be happening? Luck was certainly on Jim's side that fateful day!

A small creek fed both ponds. Casting flies was easy as there were not many bushes or trees near the shorelines. The upper pond was smaller while the lower was probably four or five times larger.

Jim and I could not believe our good fortune since most fishermen had not heard the news yet. I joined him at the ponds the following day, and we both hooked and landed several two-to-three-pound rainbow trout.

When I arrived home, I couldn't wait to tell my boys about this great fishing opportunity so close to Denver. The following Saturday, Writer, J.D., and I woke up early and drove to the ponds. If you carefully perused the water, it was relatively easy to spot large trout cruising or rising near the shoreline.

The genie was soon out of the bottle, and the news spread quickly. It took only a few days before more and more fishermen started appearing. The fishing pressure suddenly increased ten-fold. There were no signs posted on the property stating any fishing regulations so I knew most of the larger trout would probably disappear.

For a few weeks, Jim and I were able to hook many large rainbows using both dry flies, nymphs, and streamers.

Of course, the fishing pressure increased, and our catching success slowed down. We continued to fish both ponds off and on for a year or so with only moderate success.

Writer and I were fishing the ponds one afternoon when he hooked a big fish using a red San Juan Worm. He had a major fight on his hands using a lightweight Winston rod. Initially, Writer did not know what species of fish had taken his fly, but after a struggle of several minutes, it became obvious as he reeled his prize closer to shore. This fish was an exceptionally large grass carp. Writer beached his fish, removed the fly, and carefully nudged it back into the pond. The size of this carp was comparable to many of the larger trout.

Eventually, the City of Evergreen posted rules and regulations for fishing the two ponds including catch and release, limiting the number of fishermen each day, requiring check-in at the Evergreen Recreation Center, and charging a daily fishing fee of $25. These rules were too little to late to make much difference as most of the big trout were already gone.

During this time, Jim invited me to join him at a Trout Unlimited fundraiser in Evergreen where the patrons could bid on fishing equipment and other items. I noticed an Evergreen fishing card with ten punches for fishing the two municipal ponds. Placing a bid, my name was called as the winner. Both Jim and I shared my card and took turns fishing the ponds, but never completed all ten punches as the fishing was slow, and we eventually lost interest.

Jim and I were blessed with incredible fly fishing close to Denver as those two Evergreen ponds offered large rainbow trout because Jim "hit the jackpot."

Next: **Sharing a Rod**

## Chapter 17

## Sharing a Fly Rod

---

*"As the non-fishing person,*
*I would stand on the bank*
*with a better visual vantage point*
*than Jim had while wading in the stream."*

---

Fly fishing is an individual sport. When several fly fishermen arrive on the river, each one goes his own way to find a good stretch of fishable water where he can cast to waiting trout. This sport can be competitive as many fishermen keep track of the numbers and sizes of trout caught so they can brag about their fly-fishing exploits. Having two fly fishermen sharing one fly rod on a stream is a relatively alien thought. The first time for me was out of necessity.

During my second trip to Alaska, our Cessna float plane landed on a small lake near the American River. The lake didn't have enough length for the plane to take off with the weight of four fishermen on board. We deplaned and walked toward the river knowing we would meet our guide and pilot a few miles downstream at a larger lake where the plane could easily depart with four of us.

Jim and I fished different runs on the river always staying within sight of each other as there were active brown bears in the vicinity. While wading downstream and beaching a dolly varden trout, I noticed the tip of my two-piece Orvis fly rod was broken. I couldn't figure how it happened but luckily, I had brought an extra fly rod, but it was sitting back at the lodge. For all practical purposes, I figured my fishing day was over.

I walked downstream arriving at a pool where Jim was casting. Explaining my predicament, Jim suggested we take turns fishing his Orvis fly rod as we waded downriver toward the lake. He asked me to give him some tips on reading the water and where to best fish the ripples and seams with streamer flies. Taking turns casting Jim's rod, I offered him my best advice. We took real pleasure watching each other catch fish.

Our rod-sharing experience in Alaska carried over to Colorado when Jim asked me to join him for a half day's fishing on a private lease through his membership in a local fishing club called Rocky Mountain Anglers. A rod fee was charged to each member and his guest fishing a private lease. Jim phoned the club's representative to see if we could share a rod thereby reducing our cost to only one rod fee. Obtaining an approval, Jim and I arrived at a lease near Winter Park, Colorado around noon.

Ranch Creek was a classic small stream ten to twenty feet wide with cut banks and short runs winding through meadows adjoining several beaver ponds. Part of the stream with closer access to the road was occasionally stocked with sixteen inch or larger rainbows. Most of the creek was inhabited by wild German browns in the eight-to-twelve-inch range. Jim and I carefully followed the rules taking turns fishing until one of us caught a fish and then exchanging my Winston fly rod with each other. Sharing a rod was an enjoyable experience.

Sometimes when fishing our own rods, Jim and I would "flip-flop" each other while one of us fished one run and the other moved ahead to the next one and vice versa. Writer and I also fished the Ranch Creek lease and took turns hooking a dozen or so large rainbow trout stocked in the same deep pool.

Spending quality time together is very important in today's fast-paced and stressful world. Even after reading my comments, you may have doubts about sharing a rod, and it is not for everyone. Most of you will never try it. However, I believe the positives far outweigh the negatives in certain circumstances as it can provide a special fishing experience with a friend or relative. Here is to "sharing a rod."

Next: **Proud Papa**

# Chapter 18

# Proud Papa

---

*"We both watched captivated as in slow motion,*

*the parachute Adams floated toward the fish.*

*With a sudden quick swirl,*

*the trout sucked in the imitation,*

*Writer raised his rod and set the hook."*

---

**B**ack in the late 1980's and early 1990's, the fishing on the Colorado River below Parshall was especially good before the Whirling Disease decimated the rainbow trout population. The river was inhabited with many rainbows and German browns, but overall, the rainbows were the much larger fish. What made the fly fishing even better was the fact that these rainbows would readily take the dry fly. Over the summer months, the morning insect hatch included pale morning duns while the late afternoon brought caddis flies.

One morning while fishing alone on the Colorado River near Parshall at the Kempe Unit, I waded my favorite run above the bridge in the deeper current down the right side. The river was waist high, and I was wading ten or twelve feet from the cut bank. Suddenly, I lost my balance and fell onto my knees, and the river was "up to my neck." Does this remind you of a previous incident? I could not stand up because of the heavy current. There was no one to call for help. I had previously tightened my wading belt around my chest, so I was wet but not taking in much water. I could think of only one way to possibly alleviate my predicament. I lunged and threw myself forward through the water for several feet toward the bank. This maneuver worked perfectly as I was able to almost reach the shore, grabbed a low overhanging tree branch with my right hand and pulled myself to my feet. It was a close call. I was thankful that I was okay and only wet and cold. It was another lesson for me to be extra careful when wading a river especially when fishing alone.

Jim, Writer, and I have fly fished below Parshall many times. One day, Writer and I were fishing above the bridge. Writer was wading the right side while I took the left. He fished in the shade of the overhanging trees but had to be careful when casting to keep from snagging his fly in the shoreline vegetation. Writer waded upstream ten to fifteen feet from the bank. The current was slow and strong, and the water was at his mid-thigh. This section of the river was at least a hundred yards long with many small riffles and seams. It was classic dry fly water.

During a pale morning dun hatch, Writer and I were casting to rising trout. After fishing partially up the left side, I decided to leave the river and walk back across the bridge to watch Writer fish. I crossed over the bridge and moved down the shoreline until I stood on the bank above him. As Writer approached the top part of the run, he deftly cast the Winston fly rod and placed his size #18 parachute Adams softly on the water.

Noticing a large log lying just under the surface thirty feet in front of him, I spied a trout rising every few seconds just below it. I wondered if Writer could see this working trout from his vantage point. I didn't want to move closer nor make any noise which might spook it. Writer glanced up at me and pointed upriver toward the log and mouthed the words "rising fish." Wading slowly upstream, he covered a wide variety of water with his casts. Moving to within fifteen feet of the log, Writer could readily view this active trout. I felt as if I was almost joining him in slow motion as he raised his right arm, made a slow back cast, and skillfully shot the fly line forward so his parachute Adams landed gently on the water a foot above the fish. We both stared captivated as in slow motion the fly floated toward the target. With a sudden quick swirl, the trout sucked in the imitation; and Writer raised his rod setting the hook. It was a superb dry fly-fishing moment where he spotted the fish and presented his dry fly perfectly.

This rainbow trout took off downstream like a rocket moving into the deeper and faster current. The line shot off Writer's reel. There was no doubt it was an exceptionally large fish as it suddenly exploded out of the water. Both of us shouted excitedly about its size. Writer quickly waded downstream following the trout. I ran back down the bank and yelled that I would attempt to net it for him. Worrying that the rainbow trout might escape if it moved below the bridge, I climbed down into the river. I watched Writer as he skillfully fought the fish on the lightweight Winston rod. By applying constant pressure, Writer finally stopped its downstream flight. More than ten more minutes passed before I could net his trout. This rainbow was much longer than my net with a portion of its body and tail hanging out the top. Writer's big rainbow measured twenty-four inches long and probably weighed four or five pounds. This fish was a gorgeous golden-green with long dark red stripes down each side.

After the epic struggle, Writer revived the exhausted rainbow by carefully moving it back and forth in the current. He was exceptionally lucky to land such a big trout using 5X tippet and a small #18 parachute Adams.

During the years, Jim. Writer and I have caught several other large rainbow trout on the Colorado River near Parshall, but not one could compare to the trout Writer hooked directly above the log that fateful day. While fishing the Colorado River the following year, Writer, and I both looked for that same log in the river, but it was gone probably being swept downriver during the heavy spring runoff.

Due to the Whirling Disease, the larger rainbows perished and disappeared. For several years after, the river was comprised of only smaller German browns. Eventually, the Colorado Game and Fish stocked the Colorado River with Whirling Disease resistant rainbow hybrids.

My heart just swelled with pride watching my son wade, cast and catch a trophy-sized rainbow trout. This was a Kodak moment even though neither of us had brought a camera. I had witnessed a coming-of-age moment for Writer. He was a quick-learner and already an exceptional fly fisherman. I couldn't help smiling as I was such a "proud papa."

Next: **Salmon Socking**

Copyright © BestVector    Website URL: http://RetroClipart.com/123

# Chapter 19

# Salmon Socking

---

*"All of a sudden, there was a loud pop*
*across the river as Jim's line and fly*
*came shooting straight back at him."*

---

T here was a special place to fish in early October on the Western slope of Colorado. The location was near Almont, Colorado where the Gunnison, Taylor and East Rivers all converge. This is not about trout fishing, but rather about fly fishing for kokanee salmon that spawned in the East River. These salmon make a long 20-mile journey upstream out of Blue Mesa Reservoir into the Gunnison River and finally end up in the East River in pools adjacent to the Roaring Judy State Fish Hatchery. This hatchery removes five to six million eggs from the kokanee annually (about half of the state's total eggs) which are raised to two-inch fry for restocking in several reservoirs. The spawning salmon perish after making the long journey and depositing their eggs.

First, my son, Writer, was invited by a friend, Ben Day, and his father to fly fish for these spawning kokanee salmon. After experiencing this annual event, Writer enthusiastically told me about the fabulous time he had catching these fish.

It was just a year later when we packed our gear and made the four-hour drive to Almont and the East River. Even though it was during the middle of the week, there were still ten to fifteen fly fishermen packed together fishing five or six holes in one short stretch of the river. What made this scene even more remarkable was the large concentration of kokanee salmon stacked together in each hole.

The best fishing method was using weighted streamer flies of any kind. The East River is a smaller stream so long casts are not required to reach the other side. Writer and I preferred fishing size 4-to-6 red or orange streamer flies imitating an egg pattern. It did not matter what fly pattern we tied to our leaders as the salmon were not picky.

I stood within a few feet of the next fisherman, cast into the pool, and watched as my fly line moved downstream. As soon as it stopped, or I felt a bump, I raised my rod and set the hook. Sometimes these salmon took my fly in their mouths while other times I might snag one in its body. Most of these fish measured twelve to sixteen inches. The kokanee were stronger fighters than trout and jumped and cartwheeled repeatedly. All the salmon had to be quickly released since the fish were in full spawning mode. Writer and I had an amazing time hooking many fish during the afternoon and the next morning.

Since fishing for kokanee was such a fun experience, I brought my stepson, J.D., and my friend, Jim, back for this salmon run the next fall. I knew both would love the opportunity to fly fish this annual event. Spending the first night at a motel in Almont, we arrived at the East River near the hatchery early the next day.

J.D. could not believe his luck. Grinning constantly, he hooked fish after fish. He would not even take a lunch break as he did not want to lose his prime fishing spot. It was as close to fishing nirvana as J.D. could possibly imagine. He probably caught fifty to sixty salmon during a full day's fishing.

Jim and I were much more relaxed but still had plenty of action. We took more breaks and enjoyed watching J.D.'s and the other fishermen's constant action.

Later in the afternoon while watching Jim cast across the river, his fly landed in some willow bushes on the other side. His large orange streamer fly caught in the top of a bush, and he didn't want to wade across the river to retrieve it. Instead, Jim applied constant pressure to his rod hoping his fly would let loose. Suddenly, there was a loud pop from across the stream, and Jim's line and fly shot straight back at him. His streamer fly hit him directly burying its barb deeply in the right side of his neck. It was another lesson to be extra careful when pulling on a snagged fly because the outcome can be dangerous.

Jim was upset finding a large orange fly buried in his neck, but I told him not to worry as I would quickly remove it. Remembering Allan's method from the past, I cut a piece of leader tippet, placed it around the curve of the fly's hook, wrapped both ends of the tippet around my right hand, and quickly jerked the fly loose. Jim couldn't believe how easy and painless the removal process was with only minimal bleeding and a slight swelling where the barb had been stuck.

Those two trips I made with my boys and Jim to fish for kokanee salmon on the East River were especially memorable. Catching all those fish was almost too easy.

I recently read an article in "American Fly Fishing" magazine mentioning fishing for kokanee salmon is no longer allowed in the East River near the fish hatchery due to the recent drought conditions and fewer salmon in the river. There is still an opportunity to fish for these salmon during the late fall migration up the Gunnison River.

I knew I had my priorities right by spending quality time fishing with my boys and Jim. We had discovered the ultimate fishing fun, "salmon socking."

Next: **You're the Winner**

# Chapter 20

# You're the Winner!

---

*"Our female guide told us the fly fishing*
*was rated superb on this small stream*
*populated with rainbows, German browns,*
*brookies and cutthroat trout.*
*If a fly fisherman could catch*
*all four species in one day,*
*he or she would achieve*
*the Colorado Grand Slam."*

---

O ne day during the spring of 1995 while grocery shopping at a King Soopers supermarket with my wife, DeAnne, I noticed a sweepstakes box with entry forms at the customer service counter. What caught my attention was a future drawing for a free trip for two including two night's lodging and meals and one day's guided fly fishing at the Orvis Elk Trout Lodge near Kremmling, Colorado. The total package was valued at $1,200. Not being familiar with the Elk Trout, my interest was piqued so I filled out an entry form and placed it in the box.

As time passed, I never gave this sweepstakes another thought until one day a month or so later. I received a phone call from a King Sooper's manager telling me that I had won the trip. I couldn't believe my good luck. The next day, I stopped by the store and picked up the free trip certificate and a brochure for the Orvis Elk Trout Lodge. I was excited to take advantage of this extraordinary fly-fishing opportunity.

The Elk Trout Lodge consisted of a great room with high ceilings and a fireplace, a kitchen, dining room, eight two-person guest rooms, and two four-person guest cabins. A chef prepared delicious meals for the guests. This resort was an exclusive Orvis fly fishing venue which included private fly-fishing leases on the Blue River, Troublesome

Creek, the Colorado River, and several lakes and ponds nearby. Best of all, there was the possibility of catching a trophy-sized trout.

This free trip had to be booked during the last weekend of October and on the final day of guided fishing at the resort. I would pay the normal gratuities for the guides, staff, cooks, and housekeeping services as well as any fishing flies I might purchase from our guide.

My son, Writer, who was attending Colorado College in Colorado Springs, loved the opportunity to join me so we departed on a late October afternoon for the Elk Trout. Being in high spirits, we made the easy one-and-a-half-hour drive to the lodge located near the small town of Kremmling. It was situated on a bluff overlooking a picturesque, lush valley with the Colorado River below.

After arriving, Writer and I were situated in a second-floor guest room with an attached bath. The first night, we enjoyed a delicious steak dinner and dined with ten other guests. With a maximum capacity of twenty-two guests, the lodge was less than half full during the last day of the season. A few guests were staying at the Elk Trout to hunt ducks and geese in blinds on the rivers and ponds nearby.

The next morning Writer and I arose early, ate a hearty breakfast, and were excited and "raring" to start fly fishing. The day was cool, cloudy, and raining lightly. A young female introduced herself as our guide and drove us to a couple of small ponds adjacent to the Blue River. We put on our rain jackets and started casting our Winston rods with parachute Adams attached near the shore. While it continued to rain, suddenly the water started boiling with fish rising everywhere. Considering all the action, I thought we would hook fish after fish, but it was not to be. Writer and I both managed to catch a couple of brown trout, but before we knew it, our time was up so we packed up our gear, and our guide drove to the nest lease.

When concentrating on fishing, I rarely pay attention to time, but an hour and a half goes by far too quickly especially when there is good fishing activity. Our guide explained to us that each leased property is fished for only an hour and a half so that all the fishermen have an equal opportunity to spend time at the Elk Trout's five best leases. Both Writer and I found switching properties often was frustrating since it seemed like we would have to depart just as soon as we began to catch trout.

The second lease was located on a high plains ranch where there was a long narrow lake with scrub brush growing around the shore. Writer and I spread out and fished weighted streamers casting as far as possible into the lake, letting our lines sink, and retrieving our flies with short, stripping movements. I was the first one to hook a good-sized rainbow. After a difficult fight, our guide netted and measured my fish at 22 inches. She took a photo of me holding my trophy, and quickly returned it to the water.

It was just a few minutes later when we heard a shout from Writer. He was hooked up with another large trout. Our guide ran quickly down the shoreline to assist him, but before she could reach him, the trout made a jump, threw the fly and was gone.

Soon, it was time to depart for third lease. After a short drive, we arrived at Troublesome Creek, a small, beautiful stream with undercut banks winding its way down toward the Colorado River through green meadows and a high bluff on one side. Our guide parked her vehicle adjacent to the creek, and we relaxed while eating our lunches. She said fishing was rated superb on this small stream populated with rainbows, German browns, brookies and cutthroat trout. If a fly fisherman could catch all four species in one day, he or she would achieve the Colorado Grand Slam.

Troublesome Creek was easily wadable, and both Writer and I caught several beautifully marked trout on a parachute Adams in the twelve-to-sixteen-inch range. Due to the ninety-minute time limit, catching all four species eluded us both. This was the one lease we both wanted to fish longer, but soon, it was time to move again to the next location.

The fourth lease was situated next to a road that paralleled Troublesome Creek. It consisted of two small deep ponds. The day was sunny and warm, and our catching luck had slowed down. I hooked one large trout but quickly lost it while Writer was shut out.

The last lease was located on the Colorado River near where Troublesome Creek entered the river. It was late afternoon, and since Writer had more energy that I did, he waded fishing upstream. There were no fish rising, but I continued to fish my Winston rod using a parachute Adams and a bead head pheasant tail dropper. My enthusiasm quickly waned since I was tired from our long day, so I quit fishing and sat down on the bank, relaxed, and enjoyed the view. Writer's perseverance paid off as he successfully hooked and landed several trout but nothing exceptionally large.

Our guide drove us back to the lodge so we could take showers and change our clothes before dinner. We thanked her for showing us a successful fishing day. That evening we enjoyed another delicious meal. Unbeknownst to either Writer or me, the lodge had a dinnertime tradition where the fishing guides recognized the largest trout caught that day.

The Elk Trout had a "21-inch Club" so I was acknowledged along with two other fishermen who had landed a fish over twenty-one inches. Our awards included a small trout hat pin as well as having our names inscribed on a wall board in the dining room and in the "Elk Trout Big Fish Book."

Our one day's fishing experience at the Elk Trout was enjoyable and educational. Writer and I learned how the lodge and guides operated. We were able to fish five private properties and caught some beautiful trout. Our guide was knowledgeable and took good care of us. I would rate the fishing as fair because the time constraints effected our success. After a good night's sleep, Writer and I joined everyone for a delicious breakfast, paid our gratuities, thanked our hosts and guide, and left the lodge around 9am.

While driving parallel beside the Colorado River toward Parshall, Writer and I decided to stop at the Kempe Breeze Unit and see if our favorite fishing spot above the bridge was available. Since it was a cool and overcast day, we both thought our chances of catching trout looked favorable. After parking our car, we put on our waders, strung up our Winston rods with a parachute Adams and a green bead-head copper John dropper, walked rapidly upstream to the bridge, and looked over the river. Nobody was fishing, and trout were already rising in the riffles.

Our favorite wading locations were just waiting for us. It didn't take long before Writer and I hooked trout. We enjoyed a marvelous three hours on the river catching and releasing at least a dozen or more brown trout each. None were particularly large averaging twelve-to-fifteen inches, but the fishing was much better on this public water than the Elk Trout's private lease on the Colorado River. To be fair, Writer and I had an advantage since we were fishing our favorite water with a good hatch and no time constraints. It was a wonderful ending to a successful trip.

Unfortunately, the Elk Trout Resort has closed its doors and is no longer in business. Still, there is nothing quite like the rush I felt when hearing those words, "You're the winner."

Next: **Monsters of the Deep**

# Chapter 21

# Monsters of the Deep

---

*"Matt held his boat in neutral*
*while he netted each fish,*
*and then rowed back upstream.*
*against the current*
*until he was in position*
*to take us down*
*through the same hole."*

---

D riving down I-25 toward Casper, Wyoming early one morning in May, Writer and I were looking forward to meeting our fishing guide, Matt Johnson, and flyfishing Grey's Reef, a special stretch of water located on the North Platte River. Our first night was spent in a motel in Casper. The next day, we were up before daylight, ate a hearty breakfast, and drove to the small burgh of Alcova. We could hardly wait to start our day's float trip flyfishing for trophy-sized trout.

The North Platte River flows out of a dam below Alcova Reservoir and is full of freshwater shrimp. The trout gorge themselves on these crustaceans and grow quickly into huge, heavy, football-shaped fish. The river is flushed-out every spring with heavy flows which provide excellent gravel beds for spawning fish. It has all the ingredients to maintain a prolific trout population. Most of the river is surrounded by private ranches with hardly any public water. The best method to fish the river is by floating downstream in a McKenzie drift boat and casting to trout with tiny nymphs. The bigger fish are congregated in the first mile or so in deep holes.

Our guide, Matt Johnson, had been an All-American wrestler in college at Iowa State University and later was an assistant wresting coach at the University of Wyoming. He is a very positive and friendly person. Matt is knowledgeable about the North Platte River and provides his personally tied tiny nymphs. Being extremely strong with highly developed back, leg and arm muscles, he can easily row his boat using just one hand moving upstream against the heavy current while keeping us fishing the most productive runs over and over. When fishing with Matt, everyone catches trout and has a great time.

This was my second opportunity to fly fish this stretch of river with Matt since my friend, Jim, and I had joined him for a similar float trip a few years earlier. That trip, also in May, was cold, windy, and rainy. Jim and I had to laugh as we remembered that special day. Our fly rods were not stout enough for these big rainbows, so Matt worked quickly and diligently setting up two of his rods and reels with new leaders, yarn indicators, split shot, and several small nymphs. Just as he was ready to launch his McKenzie drift boat, Jim and I noticed that our leaders had tangled together. Even with the windy conditions, it was still our fault as we didn't keep our rods separated to avoid a tangled mess. Nothing bothered Matt as he just smiled, laughed, and kidded us about getting ourselves in such a tangled predicament so soon after he rigged us up. He patiently and quickly untangled our leaders and flies. This same process would have taken Jim and I much longer, and probably out of frustration, we would have cut off the tangled mess and started over again.

While moving down the river, Matt covered only the most productive water which was less than a mile or so from our launch point. After floating the short upper portion of the river, he pulled his boat out of the water, walked back the mile to get his truck and trailer, picked up his boat, drove us upstream to our original starting location, and rowed us again and again through the most productive fishing sections during the afternoon. I have never witnessed a guide like Matt who worked so hard and went to much trouble to provide Jim and me with the best trout fishing possible. Going the extra mile for his paying customers is second nature to Matt. He showed his incredible knowledge, strength, and perseverance. Matt's skills as a guide are unmatched. With his tutelage, Jim, and I each caught several large trophy-sized trout.

It was a year later in May, when Writer and I joined Matt at Grey's Reef. Writer was fishing his own ten weight Scott rod while I borrowed one of Matt's stouter fly rods. The morning was gorgeous, warm, and partly cloudy, and best of all, there was no wind. We expected the wind to pick up as the day progressed. Matt expertly rigged up our fly rods with leaders, orange yarn indicators, his tiny nymphs, and split shots so our lines and flies would sink down at least three or four feet. There was no doubt that we were going to be nymphing the deeper pools for huge trout.

Outfitted in our chest waders, boots, and fishing vests, we helped Matt launch his McKenzie drift boat into the river. As soon as the boat moved away from shore into deeper water, he told us to cast our flies off the right side of the boat since there was a deep hole near shore. Writer was in the front of the boat while I positioned myself standing in the back. It is not easy to cast heavily weighted leaders, but Writer and I shot our lines out ten feet away from the boat and focused on our orange yarn indicators slowly bobbing and moving with the current.

Our flies had not been in the water for more than thirty seconds, and the boat was approximately ten feet from shore when Writer's indicator jerked under the water. He raised his rod setting the hook. A huge rainbow trout exploded out of the water in front of us, and we all shouted with excitement about the sheer size of this fish. Writer could not believe his good luck. I quickly reeled in my line and watched while he struggled fighting this monster. Matt used his oars to deftly navigate the boat providing Writer with the best advantage to fight and land his trout. It took at least ten minutes before he finally won the battle, and Matt netted this trophy-sized rainbow. Writer looked in amazement at this beautiful rainbow trout which measured about 25 inches long and weighed at least six to eight pounds. I took a photo of Writer holding his king-sized fish and watched as Matt carefully slid it back into the river. It was an auspicious way to start to our float trip!

Matt knew the North Platter River and Grey's Reef so well. Rowing his boat downstream through a good run, Writer, and I both hooked trout almost simultaneously. Matt held his boat in neutral while we struggled fighting these monsters. He netted each fish, and then rowed back upstream against the current until he was in position to take us once again down through the same hole. Matt was phenomenally strong and would repeat this same feat three or four times in a row while Writer and I caught more king-sized trout. Almost every time Writer or I would see our indicators move, we would raise our rods setting the hooks and sure enough, we had hooked another rainbow.

The first mile of the river below the dam at Alcova contained the best habitat for holding big trout. There is almost no dry fly action on the river so deep nymphing is the method of choice. We caught far fewer trout in the afternoon while slowly floating the last five or six miles to the take-out location.

It was another spectacular day's fishing on Grey's Reef. Both Writer and I each hooked and landed ten exceptionally huge trout. Everything came together to make this the perfect fishing day. First, having no wind on the North Platte River in May was unbelievable. Second, Writer and I were fishing with the best guide, Matt Johnson. Third, Writer caught the largest trout on his first cast. And finally, every trout we caught was large. If only we could have bottled our day on Grey's Reef and saved it for another time. Writer and I relished every moment after spending a phenomenal day with our top-notch guide, Matt Johnson, while fishing for "monsters of the deep."

Next: **The Whirlpool**

*Hooked by Fly Fishing.*          Graham M. Mott

© CanStockPhoto.com

# Chapter 22

# The Whirlpool

---

*"The fish continued hitting the surface*
*and splashing near our boat.*
*It was truly an amazing experience*
*blindly raising our rods*
*and hoping to hook a trout."*

---

In the early spring of the year 2000, my friend, Jim, called me and mentioned that he had met a man named Al who lived near him in Evergreen, Colorado and was a partial owner of a fly-fishing lodge in British Columbia, Canada. He suggested we visit Al at his home and see if we had any interest in pursuing a fishing trip. The thought of fly fishing in British Columbia intrigued me. Not long afterwards, Jim and I stopped by Al's home and talked to him about his lodge and the flyfishing possibilities. He gave us brochures and mentioned four rivers that produced superb rainbow trout fishing. Guides could float us on the "World Famous" Horsefly River, Quesnel River, Cariboo River, and Mitchell River. The wild rainbow trout would average between 17-to-24 inches which sounded "too good to be true."

There were a few available calendar dates during mid-summer for four days of guided fishing. I mentioned this trip to my son, Writer, and he loved the idea of joining us. It was not long before Jim, Writer and I booked a summer fishing trip to Al's lodge in British Columbia. We felt it had all the ingredients for another exceptional fly-fishing experience.

Everything looked good when we boarded our flight from Denver to Vancouver on July 29th. Our plane arrived in Canada thirty-five minutes late. Jim, Writer, and I had less than an hour of layover time to make a commuter plane flight to Williams Fork, British Columbia. By the time we made through Canadian customs, picked up our bags and rods, and ran for the gate at the other end of the terminal, our plane had just departed.

Obviously, we were in a tough bind with the possibility of losing a full day's fishing since there was only one daily flight to Williams Fork. Of course, this dilemma reminded Jim and I of our previous trips to Montana when we lost fishing days due to Frontier's incompetence. Could this happen to us again?

After talking with an airline's employee regarding our predicament and venting our frustration, he suggested taking a later commuter flight farther north to the town of Prince George. We could rent a car, drive an hour and half to the Williams Lake airport, leave the rental car, phone the lodge, and have someone drive us to the Northern Lights Lodge. This was our only option if we wanted to be fishing the next day.

Our flight to Prince George went without a hitch. Writer drove us in a rental car on a scenic drive through the countryside paralleling a river to the Williams Fork Airport. Upon our arrival, I phoned the lodge from a pay phone, and we waited a couple of hours for one of the owners to pick us up. We finally arrived at the Northern Lights Lodge at 9pm, and it was already dark outside. We were tired but happy after our long day's ordeal. There was no doubt we would be ready to go fly fishing early the next morning.

Northern Lights Lodge is located on the shore of Quesnel Lake. The main lodge was built of cedar logs in 1942. It has a common room with a vaulted ceiling, a huge stone fireplace and eight guest rooms accessed by a wrap-around deck with breathtaking views of the lake.

Shortly after our arrival, we were introduced to another fisherman named Jon who would be joining our fishing group. He was a stockbroker from Denver, had no fly-fishing experience, and was going to be Jim's fishing partner for the next four days.

The next morning was a beautiful warm summer day. We rode in a jet boat across Quesnel Lake, which is the deepest freshwater fjord in the world stretching seventy-five miles from end to end. After arriving on the far shore, we were picked up by two local fishing guides who drove us to the "World Famous" Horsefly River. The Horsefly is best known for having a large salmon run in the late summer and fall. In fact, the whole Quesnel watershed is noted for hosting one of the largest sockeye salmon populations in the world.

The Horsefly River could be described as medium-sized with deep holes and reminded me somewhat of the Colorado and Gunnison Rivers.

Writer and I started fishing out of a McKenzie drift boat while Jim and Jon would be riding in a much larger pontoon boat which was not ideal for flyfishing. During the morning, Writer and I cast our Winston rods and royal Wulff dry flies close to the shoreline but only attracted tiny trout, perhaps only two-to-four inches long that kept nudging our flies. I hooked a bigger fish behind a rock while floating down the middle of the river but unfortunately lost it before getting a good look at its size. It might have been the big fish of the day, but there was no way to prove it. No one had any luck catching trout during the morning.

After a shore lunch, we decided to switch boats and partners. I joined Jon and his guide on the pontoon boat while Jim and Writer launched themselves in the drift boat. Their boat moved across the stream toward rising trout in some eddies and riffles. I watched enviously as Writer and Jim hooked and landed a half dozen small to medium-sized rainbows. I hoped it was a sign that fishing was improving but was not prophetic as those few moments were the day's best fishing.

Moving downstream in the larger pontoon boat, Jon, who was shirtless, fished streamers and practiced his casting. Several times, I yelled at him to set the hook and despite his clumsiness, he still managed to hook and land one trout. I quickly lost my enthusiasm while attempting to cast from this oversized boat. My only catch of the day was an odd-looking fish called a chub.

Writer caught the most trout during our first day, but overall, the fishing was poor. For us, the "World Famous" Horsefly River was a bust and did not live up to the hype for superb rainbow fishing. Our guides were inexperienced and not knowledgeable about the river or flyfishing. It was obvious to us that they had not guided many fly fishermen. Our first day's fishing experience was not a great start to our fly-fishing trip in British Columbia.

The next three fishing days were spent floating and wading the Quesnel River. It was a wider, deeper, and larger river than any in Colorado. Our guide was named Gordy, who told us he was part Indian and spent most of his time guiding hunters in the fall. This reminded Jim and I of our previous experience with Denny Thompson who was a hunting guide taking us fishing in Alaska.

Gordy told us a story about one of his previous big game hunts when he was attacked by a black bear that charged his horse and knocked him out of the saddle during the collision. Fortunately, he survived the fall but broke his back and was in severe pain while laying across his saddle during the long horseback ride back to the lodge.

On the second day, Gordy drove us to the Quesnel River where we boarded his large jet boat. Obviously, this trip was offering us several different types of rivercrafts. His boat was maneuverable and fast and could easily go up and down the river in heavier, deeper currents. From time to time, Gordy would park the boat in shallow water while Jon, Jim, Writer, and I climbed out and waded close to shore while fishing large streamer flies.

At one location, Writer was the lucky one who hit the fishing bonanza. He found many fish rising and using a parachute Adams, caught trout after trout. None were large, but the action was continuous for an hour or so. During the afternoon, I asked Gordy to drop me off near Writer, and I also caught several fish. Our second day's success was much better.

The third day, Gordy took us back to the Quesnel and parked his jet boat near a long sandbar where the river split into two separate channels. Jim, Jon, Writer, and I waded along the edges on both sides and cast into the deeper current using nymphs and streamers catching a few trout.

After lunch, Gordy drove his boat downstream to the same location where Writer had caught so many trout the day before. He dropped Writer and me off and took Jim and Jon further downstream to try fishing some new locations.

Just like the day before, Writer and I had a ball watching trout rise and take our parachute Adams. Two hours later, Gordy drove his jet boat back upstream against the heavy current and picked us up. While downstream, Jim and Jon caught a few trout on streamers but couldn't match our success.

While back at the lodge before dinner, Gordy stopped by our room and asked if we would like to float that evening on the Quesnel River below the lodge where it leaves the lake and moves downstream. He thought there could be excellent dry fly fishing in the evening. We loved this new opportunity to fish a different fork of the Quesnel. Gordy said he would float us in a McKenzie drift boat while his friend would take Jim and Jon down the river.

After dinner, we drove to where the river leaves the lake and helped both guides put their boats into the water. Jim, Jon, and their guide left ahead of us and crossed the river toward the opposite bank. The Quesnel was wide and slow moving. While floating peacefully downstream, we spotted

Jim and Jon on the far side of the river with one of their flies snagged in a tree.

Gordy rowed his boat downstream while approaching some narrow rapids. Navigating his boat was trickier through this part of the river as there was a small drop-off and more heavy rapids ahead. Gordy made it look easy as he flawlessly rowed over the drop-off and down through the faster whitewater.

It was not long before we moved into a slower, riffled portion of the river where trout were rising rapidly all around us. The water seemed to be moving in a circular motion. There was an insect hatch, but since it was getting dark, we could not see what kind of bugs were floating on the water. Using size #16 royal Wulff dry flies, Writer and I cast quickly and as often as possible to rising trout and caught several rainbows in the twelve-to-fifteen-inch range. We were having so much fun and kept laughing and yelling about our good fortune. Time passed quickly, and soon we could no longer see our flies floating on the water. The fish continued to hit the surface and splash near our boat. It was truly an amazing experience raising our rods blindly and hoping to hook a trout. Writer and I caught a few more fish as Gordy rowed his boat in a circle. It felt as if we were in a whirlpool filled with working trout which provided an incredible fly-fishing experience.

Later that evening after loading our boat and equipment on Gordy's trailer, we met Jim, and Jon along the road. Unfortunately, their guide had played it safe and stayed above the rapids and never found the superb fishing action. Jim and Jon caught a few trout but missed the evening's best fishing activity. Writer and I downplayed our good luck so they wouldn't feel bad about their own experience.

The last day of guided fishing, Writer and I spent a relaxing day on Gordy's jet boat by ourselves. Jim's wife, Candy, had arrived, and Jon was leaving the lodge to fly back to Denver. We explored some new spots on the Quesnel and a branch of the Cariboo River nearby but did not catch many trout.

While fishing the Horsefly and Quesnel Rivers, we rarely saw any other fishermen and never caught an eighteen-to-twenty-four-inch rainbow. Jon learned how to fly fish. Jim, Writer, and I hooked plenty of trout and loved the natural beauty of the Canadian countryside, lakes, and rivers. I would recommend fishing in British Columbia at the Northern Lights Lodge but would schedule a trip in the fall to fish for sockeye salmon and steelhead trout. What made our trip was that spectacular evening's fly fishing to rising trout as Gordy rowed his drift boat in "the whirlpool."

Next: **In the Zone**

# Chapter 23

# In the Zone

---

.

*"I didn't fish for over 15 minutes*
*while watching J.D. make cast after cast,*
*hook multiple trout and release them all.*
*It was perfection on a trout stream."*

---

As you already know, many of my best flyfishing experiences have come spending time with my boys. Anytime I could fish with my stepson, J.D., I took the opportunity.

J.D. is six feet four inches tall and quite an imposing figure next to me at five feet, ten inches. After college, he moved to Phoenix to follow his dream of becoming a PGA golf pro. When visiting Denver one August day, I took him fly fishing. Using Writer's membership in Rocky Mountain Anglers, we were going to fish a private lease on Clear Creek below Georgetown Lake.

I had previously fished this same property and had a truly unique experience. This time, I noticed an odd-looking trout rising in a pool under a brushy cut bank above a bridge. I cast my Winston rod using a size #18 parachute Adams and watched it float under the overhanging bushes. Sure enough, a whitish-creamy colored fish rose and grabbed my fly. When I netted this trout, I could hardly believe my eyes as it was such an amazing sight. This oddly colored fish must have lost its color pigment. I quickly released this fourteen inch "albino" trout so another fisherman could have a "wow" moment.

It was early on a beautiful crisp, sunny day in October with the aspen trees' leaves turning a gorgeous golden yellow when J.D. and I arrived at this Clear Creek property for several hours of fishing. Standing nearby in the stream, I watched J.D. intently as he cast the Winston rod with a size #18 parachute Adams and a red bead-head copper John dropper just above the downstream property line. With a cast close to the opposite riverbank, he caught a beautiful ten-inch German brown trout. I followed J.D. while casting to riffles along narrow, brushy sections of the creek which was low and clear.

By the time we had waded the half mile or so of private water, J.D. and I already had a productive day hooking and releasing several quality brown trout. When we finally waded to the upstream boundary of the property, our only choice was to go back downstream, and re-fish the same runs we had waded through earlier in the day. Strands of barbed wire were strung across the stream at each end of the property line with signs stating the club's name, private property, and no trespassing.

While observing the stream above the property line, I looked longingly at a wide run directly ahead of us. On the right side, the stream carried around a large boulder and fanned out into slower water.

The current next to the rock was fast and deep, and there was a seam of riffles directly below for ten to fifteen feet. On the left, the stream was deeper and slower. These elements provided excellent holding water for trout, and I noticed a trout rising on the right side near the boulder.

Even though this inviting stretch was not part of the Club's property, I decided this public water was too good to pass up. We waded upstream, held up the barbed wire for each other, and ducked underneath. J.D. set up on the right side of the seam below the boulder. On his first cast, I watched as a fish immediately attacked his dry fly, and he set the hook. I didn't fish for over fifteen minutes while viewing J.D. make cast after cast, hook multiple trout, and release each one. It was perfection on a trout stream. By the time he finally made a cast and didn't hook a fish, I realized something special had happened. J.D. had made seven straight casts catching a trout each time. To say I felt proud was an understatement as I relished every moment of his success. It was rather ironic that our best fishing was on public property and not the private lease.

I surmised that a few trout stocked on the private property had probably moved upstream into the public water we were fishing. After wading downstream, J.D. and I crossed back under the barbed wire, stepped out of the creek, and walked to my car. We decided to exit the property as there was nothing left for us to accomplish. I kept pinching myself as I wondered why I had been so fortunate to be part of J.D.'s unforgettable fishing day. I don't know if he caught the significance of what had occurred. Catching seven fish on seven straight casts was a rare feat. I can vouch that J.D. was definitely "in the zone."

Next: **Lady-in-Waiting**

# Chapter 24

# Lady-in-Waiting

---

*"While I was fishing,*
*she felt completely cut off from civilization*
*sitting by herself with her only companions*
*being the chipmunks playing nearby."*

---

T hrough a business investment, I was offered a time share in Snowmass, Colorado for ten years. After that period passed, my ownership reverted to the corporation owning the development. My week included the Labor Day weekend which was a quiet time in the mountains as the summer was almost over and ski season several months away. It was a beautiful time to visit as a few leaves on the trees were beginning to change color, and the rivers and streams were running low and perfect for dry fly fishing. I always looked forward to trying my luck fishing the Fryingpan River, the Roaring Fork River, and the Crystal River.

There was always one major dilemma. This involved my beautiful wife, DeAnne, who had no interest in fishing. She enjoyed making the trip with me to Snowmass and visiting the towns of Glenwood, Aspen, Roaring Fork, and Basalt but did not like staying at the resort while I took the car and was gone for a day's fly fishing.

A fisherman's wife can have a lonely existence with her husband's total focus on his activity. What could I do to make this circumstance manageable for both of us? I carefully looked at all the alternatives so I could find some answers to create a win-win situation.

Here is what I discovered. The best remedy was to alternate fishing days. I could fish one day and during the next one, DeAnne and I could sightsee or shop. Still hanging over my head was the problem of how to occupy DeAnne while I was fishing. I thought long and hard about the best way to make this dilemma amenable to both of us.

DeAnne has insomnia, sleeps late, and moves slowly during the morning. Being impatient while waiting for DeAnne to get ready was frustrating as I am a morning person. I wanted to arrive at the Fryingpan River early to claim one of my favorite fishing spots.

Both of us operated by totally different wavelengths. DeAnne did not wear a watch and paid no attention to time. The more I pushed her to get ready, the slower she seemed to move. DeAnne and I have had this time struggle in our relationship since I first met her. She does not get ready until the last minute before attending concerts, shows, or other events. I am just the opposite as I want to arrive early for all appointments.

As far as her joining me for a day's fishing, I was already exasperated over losing valuable fishing time. We always arrived at the river mid-day or later. My best method of dealing with my feelings was to take deep breaths and make sure DeAnne was well taken care of when we finally reached our destination. No matter what I said or did, I could not cajole her to get ready more quickly.

Here were my remedies for making DeAnne's time sitting next to the stream enjoyable while I flyfished nearby: First, I bought two delicious sandwiches for lunch. Second, I set up a folding chair for her in a comfortable spot. Third, I brought her favorite books and magazines. Fourth, I provided an umbrella to shade her from the sun or in case of a rain shower. Fifth, I included a water bottle and snacks of her choice. And last, I gave DeAnne the car keys in case she had to take cover during a thunderstorm. I felt sure I had covered all the bases. Did I do enough to make DeAnne's time pleasurable while sitting by the river?

When DeAnne was settled, I hurriedly put on my waders, strung up my Winston rod, tied on an Adams parachute and a green bead-head copper John, waded in the river, and started casting. Letting my previous frustrations disappear as the water flowed around me, my total concentration was now focused on watching my floating fly. Finally, I was in seventh heaven!

Once I was fishing, I rarely looked at my watch. Time meant nothing to me as I was in a totally different space. Fly fishing is a great de-stressor for me. I could zone out for three, four, or five hours without taking a break.

*Hooked by Fly Fishing.*          Graham M. Mott

Almost nothing except lightning and a heavy thunderstorm would make me leave the river.

DeAnne always waited patiently for me to show up in a "reasonable" amount of time. As I waded up the river, did I give her any thought while I was fishing? My answer was no since I was totally oblivious to her. Was fishing for hours being insensitive to my wife?

As you know, there is always give and take in any relationship. Overall, DeAnne was a good sport even though she still complained about having to sit for hours while I fished. I knew there would always be a price to pay so I would take her out for a delicious meal or shopping during the next day.

DeAnne isn't athletic, loves books and people and has no interest in sports. While I was fishing, she felt completely cut off from civilization sitting by herself with her only companions being the chipmunks playing nearby. It is doubtful she ever saw me catch a trout. She is a wonderful person and despite our time differences, I love her very much. I can visualize DeAnne patiently sitting by the river calmly reading a book as my "lady-in-waiting."

Next: **A Fishy Tail**

*Hooked by Fly Fishing.*　　　　　　　　Graham M. Mott

# Chapter 25

# A Fishy Tale

---

*"And when it comes to fishing,
many of us have fished illegally
on private or posted property."*

---

F or about seventeen years, my family and I lived in the suburb of Littleton southwest of Denver. It was a picturesque townhome development, Columbine Lakes, located around three small ponds on the property which were fed by a small creek. Over the years, all three ponds had been stocked with warm water fish such as bass, crappie, blue gill, grass carp, and catfish. If you were lucky enough to hook a larger catfish or carp, it was great fun to try to land one using lightweight fishing gear.

Living around these ponds made it a great place to raise kids, especially J.D and Writer. We had all the advantages of living in the city and yet, could walk out our back door during the spring through the fall and catch warm water game fish. It was fun to use a fly rod and a popper to attract a bass to strike or a small dry fly to take a crappie or a blue gill on the surface.

One year, the homeowner's association stocked a few rainbow trout in the middle pond, but since the ponds were shallow with warm water during the hot days of summer, it was impossible to sustain those fish.

The maintenance manager of the homeowners' association, Charlie, lived on the property and took great pride in the ponds and "his fish." He was an avid fisherman himself. I remember him telling me that he would fish public lakes and ponds nearby and catch bass, crappie, bluegill, and catfish, and transfer the live fish in water-filled buckets to the ponds.

One hot summer day, J.D., and his friend, Jeremy, hooked a large grass carp but unfortunately, after a long battle, the fish died. Charlie was incensed over losing such a valuable prize and punished both boys by making them do community work for a few days.

Several nights during the summer, Writer and I fished for catfish using pieces of liver or hotdogs as bait. If you hooked a catfish, you were in for a real battle. One of my wife's nephews, while visiting from Iowa, put down his spinning rod on the bank one evening while he took a bathroom break. Arriving back at the pond, his rod had disappeared being pulled into the water by a catfish.

On one occasion, I noticed poachers arriving at night to fish the ponds carrying flashlights and fishing tackle. I decided to confront these men who were fishing illegally. It was not a good idea as they became belligerent, cussed me out, and told me to leave them alone. I had no real authority to stop their illegal activities, and the local sheriff's office was not responsive to trespasser calls since the ponds were located on private property. I realized it was not my problem to police the ponds. However, during daylight, if I happened to see a fisherman I didn't recognize, I wouldn't hesitate to ask if he lived in the development or was the guest of an owner.

There were two young boys from a nearby housing subdivision whom I had given permission to fish so long as they released all the fish. These boys were polite and always thanked me for the opportunity.

One summer afternoon while walking with my two poodles around the middle pond, I noticed three boys fishing on the other side. I walked up to them and said, "Hi boys. this is private property. Do you have permission to fish here?" One of the boys answered me in a loud confident voice, "We have an owner's permission to fish here." I answered, "Really, who is the owner?" The same boy quickly replied, "His name is Mr. Mott, and he said we could fish." Hearing those words, I wanted to laugh out loud but managed to keep a straight face. I asked, "Do you know Mr. Mott?" The nervous boys sheepishly stared at me. I said, "Do you know where Mr. Mott lives?" Another boy pointed toward a townhome and said, "I think Mr. Mott lives over there." I replied, "I know Mr. Mott personally, and he doesn't live near there."

All three boys looked guilty with their eyes focused on the ground and knew they might be in trouble. I continued talking. "It is obvious to me you have never met Mr. Mott." One boy mumbled, "We have some friends who told us Mr. Mott gave them permission to fish here."

I looked directly at each boy and said, "Well boys, I'd like to introduce myself. I am Mr. Mott." The boys' eyes grew large as they looked at me as if they couldn't believe what I was saying. I continued, "You look like good boys, and I can see you love to fish. Give me your names and phone numbers, and when you get home, tell your friends I want to meet everyone here at this pond tomorrow morning at 10 o'clock. Do you understand me?" All the boys answered, "Yes sir." They followed me to my townhome where I wrote down their information. I couldn't help chuckling to myself as the boys took off running home with their fishing rods and tackle boxes.

Sure enough, all five boys showed up for our meeting the next day. The two boys who had my permission to fish apologized for telling their friends they could also fish. I knew all the boys had learned a valuable lesson and since fishing is such a wonderful sport, I offered all the boys an opportunity to fish the ponds. I am a softie at heart especially when it comes to kids and fishing.

Almost all of us, at one time or another, have broken rules or told little white lies during our lives. Some of us have probably fished illegally on private or posted property or broken other rules. I am not advocating this kind of activity, but I know human nature and getting caught in the act is always the best lesson when you tell "a fishy tale."

Next: **Communion**

# Chapter 26

# Communion

---

*"Gary exhibited a lot of bravado
telling me that he was the best
fly fisherman in Colorado."*

---

There have been some moments in my life that touch me in a special way. One afternoon when my wife, DeAnne and I were shopping at Whole Foods in Belmar, a chance meeting took place. I was wearing a light green wind jacket with the name and logo of Evergreen Fly Fishers printed on the left side. My wife and I were always friendly with store employees and would say "hi" with a smile and ask how they were doing.

DeAnne and I walked up to a tall, seasoned, handsome, white-haired security guard and started chatting with him. Introducing ourselves, we learned his name was Gary. He smiled, and after looking at my jacket, asked if I was a fly fisherman. I answered yes and asked him the same question. Gary nodded as we stared directly at each other. Later, DeAnne said it was fun to watch two alpha males checking each other out.

I asked Gary a few questions about his fly fishing experiences, and soon discovered he had fished most of the major Colorado rivers and creeks for many years. Gary was primarily a nymph fisherman but had taken trout by every method and caught some trophy-sized fish. Recently, he had retired as a Lakewood Police Officer and now was a security guard for the store.

Gary exhibited a lot of bravado stating that he was the best fly fisherman in Colorado. I am not one to brag about my own exploits. I listened to his stories and discovered that he also tied his own flies. I mentioned to Gary that my own experience attempting to tie flies was not very productive. Years ago, I bought fly-tying equipment and materials, took lessons, and found out I wasn't a perfectionist or detail person. I managed to tie a few larger flies but gave up the hobby as I didn't want to spend hours sitting in front of a fly-tying vise. I offered all my equipment and materials to my stepson, J.D.

DeAnne and I continued to visit the store regularly and would always look for Gary. As time went on, we met weekly, and Gary continued to tell me more fly-fishing stories. He confided to me that he had recently given up the sport. Due to a torn rotator cuff in his right shoulder, Gary found it too painful to cast his rod. I kept insisting that he should consider surgery or learn to cast his fly rod using his left arm. Numerous times, I have used my left arm to make a cast to a location where casting with my right was impossible. Gary was adamant stating he would no longer fly fish. A few weeks later, he confided to me that the major reason he was quitting fly fishing had to do with his wife's poor health and was committed to caretaking her.

Gary told me he would like to give me his fly collection. Of course, I was blown away by this generous offer but suggested he keep his flies in case he changed his mind about fishing. It was a week later when I received a packet in the mail from him containing three fly boxes filled with all his personally tied flies. There were over three hundred small flies and nymphs in sizes 18 to 24 including: brassies, copper Johns, mayflies, bars emergers, buckskins, miracle nymphs, pheasant tails, RS2s, midges, hare's ears, scuds, parachute Adams, elk hair caddis, Griffith gnats, caddis emergers, and more. What a remarkable collection. It was the mother lode of meticulously tied tiny nymphs and dry flies.

I was blown away with Gary's generosity and realized we had forged a special fishing kinship when we met regularly and talked about the sport. In return, I was able to introduce Gary to one of my favorite Colorado authors named Terry Grosz, who wrote some amazing books about his experiences catching the bad guys as a Federal Game Warden. In fact, I gave him several of Grosz's books. While spending time together, I also learned Gary preferred that his closest friends call him by the nickname "Goose" so that is how I will refer to him from now on.

Being a fly fisherman is like being a member of a unique fraternity. It is not surprising to meet another fly fisherman on a stream and have him offer helpful information about the fishing conditions and his successful fly pattern. I have returned this generosity by giving advice and flies to other fishermen.

Let me celebrate my fly-fishing buddy, Goose, who shared his bonanza of flies with me. I salute you for your generosity. How I wish we could have fly-fished together. In your honor, I have fished a few of your flies and caught trout. Eventually, I will pass most of your fly collection on to another fly fisherman. I'm sorry to say that I lost one of Goose's fly boxes which fell out of my vest pocket while fishing the Fryingpan River. I hope another fly fisherman found this bounty and is using Goose's flies to hook trout. Goose and I, like many other fly fishermen, all feel a special "communion."

Next: **My Favorite Fly Rod**

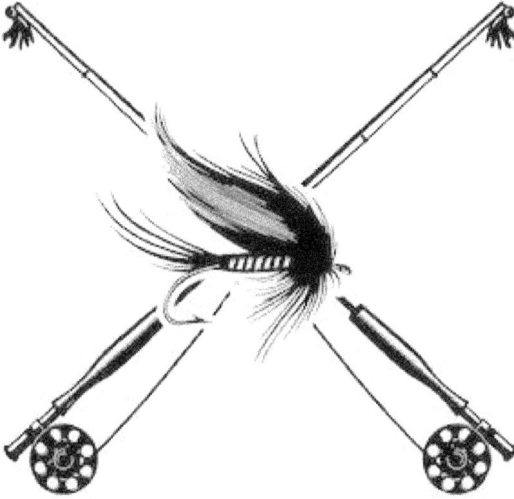

# Chapter 27

# My Favorite Fly Rod

---

*"My biggest worry is that my wife*

*(when I'm dead)*

*will sell my fishing gear*

*for what I said I paid for it."*

Koos Brandt

(I loved this quote

because it is so perfect!)

---

I want to tell you about my favorite fly rod, but first, I must mention my favorite fly patterns. Over time, I realized there is no need to have a fly box filled with many different flies. Most fly fishermen only fish their favorites.

Here are my dry flies: parachute Adams, royal Wulff, and elk hair caddis. For streamers, I suggest the muddler minnow, woolly booger, and stone fly imitation. As for nymphs, my choices are the bead-head pheasant tail, bead-head red or green Copper John, bead-head hare's ear, and caddis emergers. For dry flies and nymphs, I generally fish a size #16 or #18 and for streamers, I suggest a size #6 or #8.

My choice of fly reels includes the Orvis Lightweight, the Hardy Princess, and Ross. I enjoy fishing each one from time to time.

As you may remember, I learned to fly fish using my father-in-law's slow action three-piece bamboo fly rod. The first rod I purchased for myself was a Fenwick fiberglass rod, but with the advent of graphite blanks, my next one was the Orvis 6-foot, 5 or 6 weight "Trouter." I loved this Orvis fly rod and fished it almost exclusively for fifteen years.

One day while visiting the "Angler's All" shop on S. Santa Fe Dr. in Littleton, Jerry, the manager, suggested I take a Winston two piece 8'3", 4 weight graphite rod with a reel and line attached and cast it outside behind the building. I was truly amazed at this rod's ease of casting and laying out the fly line so smoothly. After arriving home, I told my wife, DeAnne, about this incredible rod and said I would like to own one. She decided to surprise me and purchase it for my birthday. Luckily, she talked to my friend Jim first and found out that I already had it stashed in the trunk of my car.

This Winston rod quickly became my favorite. My son, Writer, loved it too. We fished it exclusively for the past thirty years while fishing Colorado's rivers and smaller streams. I know we lost some larger fish since it is a lightweight rod, but its casting qualities are impeccable.

I broke the rod tip once and sent it back to Winston as it had a lifetime warranty. The company offered outstanding customer service, and quickly produced a new tip at no charge and repaired the original tip so I had an extra one if I ever needed it.

As I mentioned before, Writer surprised me on my birthday with a new Winston three-piece, 8'3", 4 weight rod. It is difficult to love two rods at once, but I enjoyed fishing both equally. The major advantage of owning a three-piece rod is that it fits in such a short compact case. Writer and I took turns fishing each rod as both presented the dry fly so effortlessly. My friend Jim fished one of my Winston rods and said it was a dream to cast.

Fast forward a few years and once again, I stopped by Angler's All. Jerry quickly got my attention when he told me about a new Winston fly rod he had recently cast. This one was different as it was made of fiberglass. Being a shorter 7'3" rod, it was perfect for fishing small streams. I went outside the shop, cast this slow action rod, and what happened next blew me away. I was totally in awe at how easily and softly it laid out the fly line. I never thought a glass rod could provide such perfection when casting a dry fly. Since I loved this new rod, I purchased it on the spot. Now, I was the proud owner of three Winston rods.

When I recently looked at the Winston website, I noticed that my glass rod model is sold out, but I did find one for sale on eBay. Winston is still offering several other fiberglass rods.

I know there are many excellent fly rods on the market, but if you like to fish dry flies, I recommend trying a Winston. It will be well worth your time, and you won't be disappointed.

As far as I am concerned, nothing compares to casting a Winston fly rod. I can state unequivocally that I am a

Winston fanatic and love all my rods. My fiberglass three piece is now "my favorite fly rod."

Next: **Final Thoughts**

# Chapter 28

# Final Thoughts

---

*"Fishing my fiberglass Winston rod on the clear,*
*low, and easily wadable stream with no hatch,*
*I intently watched as my parachute Adams*
*floated on the water with a red bead-head*
*copper John underneath the surface*
*and waited for an eager trout*
*to grab one or the other."*

---

211

C reating this book has been a spiritual odyssey of discovery for me. I started writing it as a journal over ten years ago for my family. Over this past year, I read my manuscript to my wife, DeAnne. She was enthusiastic and loved my stories. We decided there could be a larger audience who might enjoy reading my book. I also sent a copy of my manuscript to my sister, Sheridan, who loved my stories.

Recently, I wrote a few more chapters, an *Introduction* and an *Afterword.* Writing and editing my book has required many hours of tedious detail work, but for me, it has been a labor of love. I decided to publish my book as a paperback, eBook, and audio book.

As I mentioned previously, I uncovered and recovered my family. My book began with Hal, who introduced me to fly fishing at the Wigwam Club and eventually brought me full circle back to my father and his ancestors who were all outdoor sportsmen. I so appreciate my mother collecting and saving their stories and articles. By reading them, I realize how my father and his relatives' genes and traits fit me so well.

For a long time, I was angry toward my father over his alcoholism, but through the passage of time and reading his newspaper articles, I have forgiven him and healed myself and our relationship. My father was an exceptional writer, loved words, and always kept a dictionary close by for reference. His vocabulary was amazing. He wrote with creativity, wit, and humor.

I miss my fishing buddies Jim and Bob who have both passed away. I remember phoning Bob and reading *The Tenderfoot* chapter to him and emailed a copy to his son and daughter after his death.

Repeating the same process with my best friend, Jim, who was diagnosed with Alzheimer's, I phoned him many times and read excerpts from *Lure of Montana, Lightning Can Strike Twice* and *Trip of a Lifetime* hoping these stories might help jog his memory. Jim seemed to enjoy these chapters as he always listened quietly and thanked me. His wife, Candy, said she so appreciated my reading to him.

When talking to my friend Ken, he remembered when I floated down the Alagnac River in Alaska so I emailed him my manuscript with the chapter, *Up to My Neck* so he could relive that moment from my perspective.

I also emailed my chapter, *Monsters of the Deep*, to both Matt Johnson and his mother. She enthusiastically contacted me for complimenting Matt as my favorite fishing guide. Her whole family loved what I wrote about him because it verified what they all already knew about his talents. His Mom reminisced how Matt could out-fish her whole family when he was just a young boy. Matt phoned me recently and said that he is still doing what he loves best, spending his day's outdoors in nature and guiding fly fishermen in Wyoming.

And last, there are two other people I must mention: Allan, who taught me his easy hook extraction technique, and "Goose," who shared all his meticulously tied flies with me.

If you are not a fly fisherman, maybe you'll be motivated to try this sport. It is not easy and takes time and patience to become a competent fly-caster and catch trout. Fly fishing can lead you to self-discovery and help heal your health, emotional wounds, and addictions. If you enjoy being outdoors with nature and wading in water, it is easy to develop a love for this sport.

Fly fishing is a great de-stressor. You can totally zone out as there is no noise whatsoever except for the sound of healing water flowing around you. Best of all, you get away from cellphones, computers, and social media. If you try this sport, it is easy to get "hooked by fly fishing!"

Today, fly-fishing etiquette is especially important due to so many fishermen crowding together on public access in rivers and streams. Don't wade through another fly fisherman's water nor fish right next to him. Respect other fishermen and avoid stream or river rage.

I realize how fortunate I have been to fish so many wonderful rivers, streams, lakes, and ponds with my boys and good friends. Even though my fly-fishing days are limited as my balance is not what it once was, I now wade only in the fall in smaller, shallower streams.

I recently joined my son, Writer, for two days in late September and early October on public sections of the South Platte River near the tiny hamlet of Hartsel, Colorado. Fishing my favorite fiberglass Winston rod in the clear, low, and easily wadable stream, I peered at my parachute Adams floating on the water with a red bead-head copper John underneath the surface and waited for an eager trout to grab one or the other. On the first day, I had to laugh as both Writer and I caught and released over ten German brown trout with the longest one measuring a mere six inches. The second day, I caught the longest fish, an eight-inch brown. The size and number of trout never mattered as we relished spending our time fly fishing together.

I have enjoyed sharing my stories with you. I did not include any photos in my book because I thought it was better for you to visualize my adventures through my descriptive words. If I brought a smile to your face or you laughed at my various mishaps, I have been successful.

Here is to many more years of quiet solitude, contemplation, meditation, and contentment while fly fishing. I cannot think of a better way to tend your body, mind, and soul. The size and number of fish you catch is not important compared to the wonderful memories you make. I have so much gratitude about my life, my fly fishing experiences, and my family and friends.

I look forward to meeting you on a stream someday or in "fly fishing heaven!" These are my "final thoughts." Warmest regards,

**Graham M. Mott**


Next: **Afterword: My Family**

## Afterword: My Family

I want to tell you about my father and his relatives who were all sportsmen, hunters, and fly fishmen. I have been lucky enough to uncover and recover my family history.

My great grandfather, John. G. Mott was also called "Eagle Father." I am not sure why or how he gained that nickname. My mother told me that he owned a company in

Chicago that made wooden casks to hold various liquids such as water or booze. He was well educated. John and my great grandmother, Rue Winterbotham Mott, had two children. Their son was named Russell and daughter, Genevieve. The family had money, privilege, and social status as I have old photos of both great grandparents being finely attired to meet the King and Queen of England. My great grandfather was a big game hunter and fly fisherman. I have an original diary written in long hand by "Eagle Father" while on a month-long hunting trip in 1900 with his son, Russell, from Chicago by train to Wyoming and then by horse-driven buckboard to the Wind River Mountains to hunt primarily for elk. He was an exceptional writer and mentions flyfishing for wild trout.

Here is an excerpt from my great grandfather's diary: *I walked down to the stream, and it looked so trouty that I scanned each pool carefully in hopes of seeing a rising fish but was not rewarded by any signs of life. Going back to the fire, I asked Pixley whether there were any trout in the stream. He said, "There are no trout in Roaring Fork." I also asked if there were any falls on this river and the Green River and he answered, "No, only rapids." I knew there were trout in the Green River, and I thought there must be trout in this river also. I immediately proceeded to joint my bamboo trout rod and mounted a Royal Coachman fly. For a trial selection, I picked a quiet pool four or five foot deep at the front of an especially noisy rapid. I cast and as my fly touched the water for the third time, something shot out of the shaded depths and seized it. In a few moments, I took a beautiful half pound trout up to the fire and asked Pixley what it was. "It's the first trout I have ever heard of being caught out of Roaring Fork," he said with a surprised look. The fish did not bite well and became excessively wary, but I managed to catch three more in time to have them for dinner. The trout were silvery and black spotted. The waters of the roaring Fork flow into the Gulf of California through the Colorado River. A few days later, we were fishing on a tributary of the Snake River which flows into the Columbia River, and there the trout were darker colored with circular spots more like those of the brook trout of the East. These fish had a couple of red slashes on each side of the throat, and I suppose were of the kind commonly called cutthroat trout. I made these remarks about the trout fishing here because this was supposed to be principally a chronicle of shooting and not of fishing, and fishing will probably not be mentioned again.*

My grandfather, Russell Mott, attended Yale and became an attorney in Chicago. He hunted big game in

Canada, lower California, and Africa. I knew him slightly, when at five years old, I visited his farm near Charlottesville, VA where he and my grandmother, Helen Cutler, retired. It was an idyllic place as the countryside was so beautiful. There was a large expansive home with two servants, a cook and a farm hand who lived on the property. The property included a barn, a separate building for my grandfather's hunting rifles, antique pistols, and mounted game heads, and a kennel with many fox hounds. I remember him riding his horse attired in a long red coat blowing a horn to start a fox hunt as the dogs barked excitedly. My grandfather was an individualist and would not join the local fox hunting club. He purchased young fox pups that were let go at specific locations until they could mature and be available to hunt. His domestic dog choice was an English Bull dog named Mick. Russell wrote several hunting articles under both his own name and the pseudonym "Double Barrel" for *Forest and Stream Magazine.*

　　Russell and Helen had four children, John Grenville (my father), Evelyn, Cutler, and Joseph. Tragically, almost the whole family was wiped out by alcohol addiction. First, my grandfather died from the disease. My father, his sister, Evelyn, and his brother, Cutler, all died from alcohol abuse. Their younger brother, Joe, graduated from Yale with a law degree, married and had a child, and then committed suicide due to mental illness. My mother's sister, Lois, also died of alcoholism.

My father, who was named John Grenville Mott after his grandfather, preferred to be called Grenville. He attended the prestigious prep school, Andover Academy in Massachusetts where he played football and was president of his senior class. Later, he attended the University of Virginia in Charlottesville. My father was engaged to a woman from a wealthy family but eventually broke it off after meeting my mother who was from Terra Haute, Indiana. After college, he loved to write and became a sportswriter for a newspaper and eventually moved to New York City. My mother followed my father, and they were married by the justice of the peace in city hall. A year later, my sister, Sheridan, was born.

Since my father had chronic asthma from an allergy to ragweed, he and my mother decided to move to the desert Southwest and picked El Paso, Texas. He joined the local newspaper, the El Paso Herald Post, and wrote sports articles under his own byline, *Beyond the Pail*. In one of his newspaper articles, he wrote about betting his college tuition money on a horse race and losing it all.

*Hooked by Fly Fishing.*                    Graham M. Mott

I was born while my father joined the Air Force as a captain and was stationed in England during World War II. He went to war at 40 years old, was an intelligence officer and attended the Air Force Spy School. Most of his time in England was spent debriefing the pilots after their bombing missions to Germany. He loved his military service during the war. After returning to El Paso, he opened a successful public relations firm with two of his friends.

My father took me to many sporting events including baseball, football, basketball, boxing, wrestling, and track and field. I enjoyed it all except when he was drinking alcohol heavily which was most of the time. Of course, I remembered the events where he acted badly, became belligerent, and started arguments or fights. Those unpleasant moments made me feel uncomfortable and angry. My father never went to Alcoholics Anonymous to get help nor did my mother, sister, or I ever attend Al Anon.

It took me a long time to heal myself and forgive my father. Through reading his newspaper articles and writing myself, I eventually realized my father's alcoholism was a disease and addiction. His doctor, who was a close family friend, told him if he kept drinking alcohol he would die. I remember hoping my father would quit drinking for my sister and me, but it never happened as he could never give up the booze.

At the time of my father's death, I could not mourn his loss due to my hard feelings and anger. Many years later, I realized how much he had taught me about life and sports. Now, I can enjoy talking about him and remember the good times we spent together. I realize that I am a lot like my father being independent, outrageous and a maverick. I'm proud to say both my sister, Sheridan, and I do not drink and were able to break the cycle of alcohol addiction in our family.

What a journey I have been on, exploring my past and learning about most of my father's relatives who were writers and sportsmen. Writing this book about my fishing experiences has brought me full circle in helping me heal my anger and making me a better person. I am no longer haunted by my past. Having overcome my feelings of being ashamed, hopeless, and lacking trust, I am now self-satisfied, enjoy life, and laugh much, much more.

A recent article in *Fly Fisherman* magazine mentioned fly fishing being a good activity for people recovering from alcoholism, drug addiction, PTSD, and cancer. This sport can provide a healing outlet and help sobriety. Addicts and people who have PTSD can find a sense of purpose focusing on a wonderful sport. Men and women who are diagnosed with cancer also benefit from learning to fly fish. There are several non-profit organizations which teach fly fishing to help men and women heal from addiction, trauma, PTSD, and cancer. I recently watched an excellent new movie on Netflix, *"Mending the Line,"* which deals with fly fishing helping heal trauma and PTSD for our military personnel.

Fly fishing can help heal mental, emotional, and physical wounds as it is such a great de-stressor. It has helped me heal as an adult child of an alcoholic and brought me a sense of joy, calm and well-being.

Next: **More Information**

# More Information

**Matt Johnson**, fishing guide - 970-373-9567 (Grey Reef near Casper and Big Horn River near Thermopolis, Wy),

**Angler's All** - 303-794-1104, retail fishing store, Winston Rod dealer, 5211 S. Santa Fe Dr., Littleton, Co 80120;

**Ask about fly fishing,** flies for sale & many podcasts; www.askaboutflyfishing.com

**Budge's Flattops Wilderness Lodge** located near the White River in western Colorado.
970-536-1341, http://www.budgeslodge.com

**Casting for Recovery** (Helps women recover from breast cancer through therapeutic use of fly fishing)
109 E. Oak St., Suite 1G
Bozeman, NT 59715; toll free (888) 553-3500
www.castiingforrecovery.org

**Discount Fishing Tackle** - 303-638-2550, 2645 S. Santa Fe Dr., Denver, CO 80223

**Fly Fishers International**
5237U.S. Highway 89 S Ste 11
Livingston, MT 59047
406-222-9369, www.flyfishersinternational.org

**Fly Fishing for Conservation**
P.O Box 1192, Clovis, CA 93613; 1-559-325-7235
www.flyfishers.clubexpreess.com

**Movie:** *"Mending a Line"* about recovering from trauma
and PTSD. Available on Apple+, Google Play or Vudu

**Movie:** *"Tom"* about flyfishing and being an activist for
conservation and available on YouTube

**Nature Conservancy**
2424 Spruce St., Boulder, CO 80202,
303-444-2950,  www.preservenature.org

**Newhalen Lodge** (flyfishing destination in Alaska)
3851 Chiniak Bay Dr., Anchorage, AK 99515;
1-877-639-4256, 907-522-3355, Lodge: 907-294-2233
(summer only) www.newhalenlodge.com

**Northern Lights Lodge** (flyfishing lodge in BC)
Box 33, Likely, BC, Canada, V0L 1N0
Toll Free: 1-877-718-2200, www.nllodge.com

**Northpoint Recovery: Get Clean plus Retreats and
Addiction Treatment - Idaho & Colorado** 2335 E. State
St., Meridian, ID 83642; 208-225-8667;
www.northpointidaho.com
4565 Kendall Pkwy, Longmont. CO 80538;
855-995-4176; www.northpointcolorado.com

**Orvis:** retail stores offering flyfishing gear, flies, books, clothes, and more, www.orvis.com

**Project Healing Waters Fly Fishing** (helps Veterans with PTSD learn about fly-fishing, fly-tying and more)
P.O. Box 695, La Plata, MD 20646
1-301-830-6450
www.projecthealingwaters.org

**Reel Recovery** (free fly-fishing retreats for men living with cancer)
160 Brookside Rd., Needham , MA 02492
1-781-449-9031
www.reelrecovery.org

**R. L. Winston Rod Co.**
500 S. Main St., Twin Bridges, MT 59754
1-406-684-5674; many dealers nationwide.
www.winstonrods.com

**The Rocky Mountain Angling Club** offers memberships for fly fishing on private leases.
Rocky Mountain Angling Club, 3805 Marshall Street. Suite 303, Wheat Ridge, CO 80033
303-421-6239, 1-800-524-1814,
Email: rmangling@aol.com

**Terry Grosz**, (author and former Federal Game Warden);
His books are available at Amazon <u>and used book sites</u>:
*Wildlife Wars,*
*The Life and Times of a Fish and Game Warden. Defending*
*Our Wildlife Heritage,*
*The Life and Times of a Special Agent*
*For Love of Wilderness*
*The Journal of a U.S. Game Management Agent*
*A Sword for Mother Nature*
*The Further Adventures of a Fish & Game Warden*
*No Safe Refuge, Man as a Predator*
*Genesis of a Duck Cop, Memories and Milestones*

**Trout Unlimited**
1777 N. Kent St., Suite 100, Arlington, VA 22209;
800-284-9400; www.tu.org

**Next: About the Author**

# About the Author

Graham M. Mott was born and raised in El Paso, Texas. He is retired and lives in Lakewood, Colorado with his beautiful and loving wife, DeAnne. Graham earned a B.A. degree from the University of Wyoming He was a real estate broker for over 20 years and involved in several other jobs. Graham wrote and self-published his first book in 1993 titled, *Scams, Swindles, and Rip-offs*. At that time, he appeared on the nationally syndicated "Phil Donahue Show" and CNBC's "Steals and Deals" as well as more than 75 radio programs nationwide. His son, Writer Mott, is employed as an attorney for Arapahoe County in Denver while his stepson, J.D. Frette, owns a business, "Appliance Rescue," on Maui, Hawaii. Graham has three grandchildren, Ris Johnson, Rider Johnson, and Keen Schledorn-Mott.

9 780963 315571